Hai
1999

# FOLK
# COSTUMES
# OF THE
# WORLD

# FOLK COSTUMES OF THE WORLD

Written by Robert Harrold

*Illustrated by Phyllida Legg*

CASSELL

This book is dedicated to
Helen Wingrave
Fellow of the Imperial Society of Teachers of Dancing
who has done so much to promote folk dance and costume

Fist published in the UK 1978 by Blandford an imprint of Cassell
Wellington House, 125 Strand
London WC2R 0BB

Copyright © Blandford Press 1978, 1988; Cassell 1999
First published 1978 by Blandford Press
Reprinted 1981, 1984, 1986
First paperback edition 1988
Reprinted 1989, 1990, 1992, 1993, 1994, 1995
This revised and enlarged edition 1999
Reprinted 1999

Distributed in the United States by
Sterling Publishing Co. Inc.
387 Park Avenue South
New York NY 10016-8810

British Library Cataloguing-in-Publication Data
A catalogue record for this book is available from the British Library

ISBN 0-304-35029-X

Printed and bound in Spain by Bookprint, S.L., Barcelona

# CONTENTS

# INTRODUCTION

IN RECENT YEARS there has been a growing interest in folk costume, dance, song and music. Museums have been established in which to house costumes and examples of folk crafts, thus preventing them from being lost. Anthropologists and musicologists have travelled to remote villages to record folk songs and music or to notate dances. After many years of neglect, old instruments have been discovered and played again. Through this keen interest embroidery patterns and designs have been preserved and many costumes re-created. To understand fully how folk arts developed and the influences which controlled their development is to know a great deal of the history of a country and its people.

The basic shape evolved through the years has produced the individual costume of a country with many variations. The meaning behind so many items of clothing may well have been forgotten. The embroidery or stitching on a blouse, dress or shirt may now be merely decorative, but at one time it had a purpose or message. The wearing of a hat also had many deep and different meanings. The use of an earring or necklace could have a significance which goes back to time immemorial. People still wear their best clothes for Sundays or for religious occasions although the original purpose may well have been forgotten.

In this book the development of folk costume has been briefly outlined. Isolating the study of costume from the other folk arts can be a mistake – for example, to understand folk dance it is important to know what the dancers wear and how the costume influences the movement. Folk music can express the characteristics of a nation, their language and history. In the long flowing phrases of Russian music there is the freedom and line of their costumes. The quick rhythm of the Ukraine is shown by the short skirts of the women. The interesting rhythms of the Balkan countries find the dancers expressing the movement through their feet as their costumes often restrict the fuller use of the body.

Costume, dance, music, folklore and the decorative arts all reward study, but each subject is closely linked and a knowledge of them all gives a unifying and very full picture. To give a typical example of a costume from a country is not easy as costumes change from region to region and often from village to village. Some countries have literally hundreds of costumes and a whole book could be written on one country alone.

Costumes for work differ from those worn on Sundays, high days and holidays. For the married a different dress may be worn from that worn by the unmarried or widowed. The costumes illustrated in this book are those mainly used for dancing, either by individuals or by the various national companies and groups. For example, the Scottish costume is that for a Highland dancer and not that for rural wear, and this also applies to other countries where there is a marked difference between the costume of the dancers and ordinary wear.

Many of the costumes illustrated or mentioned are now only worn by folk dance groups, at festivals or on religious occasions. They are no longer part of everyday life.

In some of the more isolated villages in Europe, Asia and in the Americas, people still wear the costumes of the region or of their tribe. It is in these areas that old costumes, superstitions and traditions are maintained.

A visit to a village wedding in one of the Balkan countries, or a journey through Turkey, Iran, North Africa, Arabia or parts of South America enables one to see a whole wealth of costume. The wearers do not regard their costumes as fancy dress; so, if reproducing costumes for a stage performance it is essential that they should be copied as accurately as possible. There is a tendency to make them more theatrical by the addition of sequins, beads, bows or other exaggerations (unfortunately some national groups do this).

If the illustrations in this book are used as a guide in the making of costumes, it is advisable to use similar colours and materials. Some of the more striking contemporary colours may look eye-catching, but cannot give an authentic impression. Fabrics with a nylon base or with a shiny and metallic surface are not ideal as they do not hang well or move with the dancer.

Although skirts have tended to become much shorter in recent years, the illustrations in this book show the typical rather than the modern. Some dance folk festivals demand authenticity and marks are lost if there is even a slight inclination towards the theatrical.

# THE DEVELOPMENT OF COSTUME

THE BIBLE TELLS US that the first costumes worn by man were those devised by Adam and Eve. The aprons of leaves were followed by coats of animal skins so that they went out into the world in a costume still in use today.

As man travelled the world, his environment governed his costume. Natural resources and animal life were utilized and with man's development costume began to have a threefold purpose:

1  As protection against the elements, insect and animal life and adapted to the requirements of the terrain
2  For adornment, the recognition of rank and marital status and religion
3  In ritual ceremonies

All these aspects played a part in the development of costume through the ages.

Primarily a hunter, early man admired the courage and strength of the animals he killed and which provided both food and clothing. Rituals were performed by which he endeavoured to emulate these qualities by wearing their skins, and spears were ornamented with animal carvings. Religious and superstitious beliefs were linked to the wearing of special clothes.

Trees were also worshipped as a source of power and their bark and foliage were utilized in order to capture the tree spirit.

The 'Tree of Life' is often depicted in embroidery. Many tribes still plait leaves to make aprons or loincloths and the bark of trees is beaten and made into a material for clothing. In Fiji the *masi*, or bark cloth, is made by bark stripped from the trees and beaten until it is paper thin. It is then joined together and dyed and made into the *tapa* dress. The Aztec women still make a material called *ixtle* from the leaves of the maguey cactus whose tough white fibres are dyed and woven to make coarse cloth.

With the cultivation of land and the raising of cattle for food and clothing came the art of weaving. From sheep, goats, camels and llama came the wool or hair that could be utilized. In the north, the skins of caribou, reindeer, seals and the feathers and skins of birds were used. They are still used by the Lapps today. The Eskimos of the Arctic regions continue to wear all fur garments.

The native peoples of North America hunted buffalo, deer, antelope, beaver and fox for their skins and fur and sinews were used for thread. With the coming of cotton, linen, wool and silk, the basic patterns were changed.

Requiring subtropical and tropical conditions for its growth, cotton became one of the most important vegetable fibres in the world and pieces of cotton material have been found in excavations showing that it was used 5,000 years ago. Cortés received the highly prized material on his arrival in Mexico. India is the most ancient cotton-growing country and a system of hand-weaving, spinning and dyeing was in use there five centuries BC when Europe was still in a state of barbarism. China also developed cotton from very early times although not on a large scale until AD 1300. Japan followed a similar pattern.

The manufacture of cotton was to cause radical changes in costume, especially in Europe where the material was virtually unknown. It began to be produced and flourished in Spain during the thirteenth century and later spread to the Netherlands. There is some doubt as to when the industry reached England, but it might well have been brought to England during the sixteenth century when Flemish weavers fled from Spanish persecution. The USA did not begin the serious development of its cotton industry until the eighteenth century.

Following cotton came a whole range of fabrics for costumes. Calico, named after the city in India, became very popular. Corduroy and cambric were used extensively, as was fustian, the name being derived from El Fustat, a suburb of Cairo where the material was first made. Gingham was possibly derived from the Malaysian words *ging-gang*. Velveteen also came into use at this time.

Another material that came to be used extensively in making costumes was linen. The preparation and cultivation of flax was known to many ancient civilizations. In Egypt it was only the priests who were permitted to wear linen robes and it was used in the mummification of the Pharaohs.

Linen, being a stronger material, had many more uses than cotton and the growing of flax was therefore important. Ropes were made from it, with the inferior material being made into tow, some of which went into the making of wicks for lamps.

Linen could be woven into a heavy material or woven into fine cambric used for shirts and blouses. Cambric as a name came from the Flemish town of Cambrai where it was first made. It could also be used in the making of lace.

The other important textile was wool, which again had its origin far back in history. It was the Romans who taught the British the arts of spinning and weaving wool and they even set up a factory for the manufacture of clothing for the occupying forces.

In Europe the wool industry flourished and the Moors introduced the famous merino strain into Spain. England benefited from the craft of the Flemish refugee weavers who settled in the country. The Dutch introduced sheep and wool into South Africa although it did not flourish immediately. Parts of South America, Russia, Eastern Europe and Iceland all developed wool and incorporated it into their costumes. It became invaluable to those living in the mountains and in cold climates.

Although cotton and linen were known in many countries, silk was the product of only one country, China. Eventually, with the introduction of sericulture into Europe, silk played an important part in changing folk costumes. It is made from the cocoon of a special moth, which feeds on mulberries. In 2640 BC the wife of the Chinese emperor, Huang-ti, encouraged and supervized the cultivation of the mulberry tree, the rearing of the worms and the reeling of the silk. The making of the silk was a very closely guarded secret, kept by royal and noble families for many centuries; the penalty was death if the secret was divulged to others.

So prized did silk become that the famous caravan route stretching for nearly 12,800 km (8,000 miles) from China to Rome became known as 'The Silk Road'. This route carried the precious cargo from northern China into Samarkand, Bokhara and across Persia. It continued to the Tigris and Euphrates, into Syria, Egypt and Rome. This incredible journey, with its many terrain hazards and the passing of the cargo from merchant to merchant, set silk at an enormous price.

The collapse of the Chinese dynasty in the early third century made the export of silk to the West extremely difficult. The closely guarded secrets were smuggled out of China to the outside world. Japan learnt the art from four Chinese girls. It was thought to have arrived in India with a Chinese princess who hid the eggs and mulberry seed in the lining of her head-dress. From India the making of silk slowly reached Persia and Central Asia.

Justinian the Great, the most famous of Eastern Roman emperors, was most anxious to develop the manufacture of silk and he sent two monks to China. They returned with the precious eggs hidden in a bamboo cane and thus began the first Western cultivation, which started in Constantinople around AD 550.

The conquering Saracens carried the art as far as Sicily and eastward into Asia. The manufacture soon spread northwards to Florence, Milan, Genoa and Venice. In 1480 silk weaving began at Tours in France and forty years later in the Rhône Valley. Each country added its own particular features to colours, patterns and designs.

It was only in the sixteenth century that silk manufacture reached England, via the Low Countries and the Flemish weavers. The religious troubles in France nearly a hundred years later caused many skilled French Protestant silkworkers to settle in Switzerland, Germany and England. In London the weavers settled in Spitalfields and produced a silk named after this district.

Cortés tried to introduce sericulture into Mexico and James I tried to introduce it into America, but neither had much success and silk was to remain a product of the eastern hemisphere and, consequently, influence the costumes of that area.

## THE SHAPE OF COSTUME

With the development of the basic materials, peasant costume in Western Europe became established and changed only slightly from the time of the early Greeks until the fifteenth century.

The ancient civilizations of Egypt, Greece, Rome and Persia influenced the style of dress considerably, as is shown in various articles of clothing today. For both men and women the basic garment was a simple tunic, or chiton, made with or without sleeves. There were two kinds of garment, a short one called a Dorian tunic and a longer version known as an Ionian tunic. The latter was thought to have been introduced into Athens from Asia. The shorter tunic was more popular with the men and there were variations in style and materials used. For those working on the land the garment had a very simple cut. With the advance of civilization the differences in the garments of the rural and social classes became more marked. Rural workers were often referred to by the Romans as *tunicati*, from the simple *tunica* that they wore. This garment was rather like a simple shirt which reached to just above the knees or slightly higher. A form of loincloth was worn by slaves.

Women wore the long Ionic tunic made of linen with a girdle, or *zona*, around the waist. The dress was made several centimetres too long and pulled up over the girdle, which gave a skirt and blouse effect. The long skirt for the women and the short Dorian style for the men was to be the basic pattern of the peasant costume until the present day.

The changes made to this style were slight, although the fashions of the social and professional classes developed and changed continuously. The long Ionic tunic introduced from the west coast of Asia Minor bears a resemblance to the present day loose-fitting garments found in the Arab states of North Africa, the Middle East and Arabia.

The costumes of the social classes developed more rapidly and along different lines, governed by social status and rank. The peasant style remained unchanged as it met the requirements of the land workers.

Although trousers were not worn by the Greeks and Romans, they were in existence well before that period in history and were worn by the Asiatic nomadic and horsemen tribes. Tunics were not suitable for riding and consequently a short leather trouser evolved that gave both freedom in the saddle and when fighting on foot. This is worn today by the Turkish dancers when they perform the famous *kilic kalkan*, or sword and shield dance, dressed in early Ottoman military costumes. The Romans associated this form of costume with the barbaric civilizations on the outskirts of their empire and named the trousers after them. The Latin word was *bracae* or *braccae*, from which we get the English 'breeches', the Scottish 'breeks', the Breton *bragou-braz* and there are similar-sounding names in other languages. With the fall of the Roman Empire trousers were adopted by men and were made of wool, linen, leather and, in the East, cotton and silk. The materials were plain, striped or decorated with various coloured wools.

Ceaseless unrest and wars brought their changes to the various civilizations and affected costume. The male tunic was to remain, but now a form of breeches, shorts or long trousers were worn underneath. The lower leg or trouser would often be bound with strips of material and eventually the binding would become part of the lacing of the boot. The next development was the tucking of the tunic into the trouser, thus becoming a shirt.

The peasant costume of the women remained the long, simply cut, one-piece dress for many years. It was not until the fifteenth century, with the introduction of the bodice and the use of the apron, that the outline began to change. European changes of dress were slow and it was many years before the bodice became established. It is thought that the bodice was derived from a pattern worn by

Queen Marie of Anjou in the fifteenth century and this was to vary considerably. At first it was worn over the dress and was simple in design, with either a pointed or square base. Front lacing was important. The division of the figure by the wearing of the bodice eventually led to the dress becoming a blouse and separate skirt. The bodice underwent changes, straps were added and the cut and the shape altered. It became the essential part of many European costumes and there are numerous differences even in one country or region. The blouse was also to undergo changes, with alterations to necklines and sleeve lengths according to climate, fashion or religion.

It was after the French Revolution that costume in Europe began to extend in variation and styles. Social fashions changed frequently, but the rural community was slow to alter. In some parts of Europe peasants were controlled by law in the matter of dress. The laws were strictly enforced and they governed the type of material that could be used, the length of the garments, the colours and also restricted the use of decoration and trimmings. Jewellery, fancy hooks, buckles and buttons were not encouraged or elaborate dressing of the hair.

The reason for these laws was partly economic and partly religious. The Calvinistic Church feared that, without control, peasants might become extravagant in their dress or adopt fashions that could be immodest.

Governments wanted home-produced materials to be used. The social differences of the day were very marked and the upper classes did not favour peasants aping them. The French Revolution changed all this and the last of the laws were repealed. Villages vied with each other in sartorial splendour and many new ways of draping ribbons and skirts were found, with added decorations and jewellery, all bringing a wealth of new ideas.

This development coincided with the manufacture on a large scale of many new materials and designs. Many of the old ideas and traditions remained but new ideas were grafted on to them. To understand a costume fully, its history should be appreciated and the geographic features known, as all these factors have played a part in its evolution.

The difference between a working costume and one used for festive occasions is very marked. Costumes used on religious days are carefully preserved and handed down from generation to generation and are often associated with special events or traditions going back to ancient times. The animal skins and masks and the formal attire for Sundays were often thought to become impregnated either with the spirit of the animals or, indeed, the spirit of God.

## EMBROIDERY, DESIGN AND PATTERN

Every country has its own folklore, legends and myths which, through the centuries, have become more elaborate and altered. Behind many of the folk stories lies profound knowledge and truth. Those unable to express in words the powers of good and evil or light and darkness, invented signs and symbols that could be understood easily. Often between ethnic groups there are similar patterns that have a universal thread linking common designs.

Man first carved patterns on stone, metal, wood and pottery and then, later, came embroidery, weaving, carpets, architecture, etc. They could be purely decorative, offer protection to the wearer or be shapes and symbols leading to more profound thoughts.

The first form of decoration was probably in the patterns that man painted upon his body and the colours used – red, blue, yellow and white – were to represent earth, air, fire and water. The designs, apart from being for protection, also had tribal meanings. With the development of clothes, patterns were transferred to materials. Superstition and the belief in the power of evil led to cosmic symbols being used wherever there was an opening in a garment. Embroidery was used round the neck and openings in shirts and blouses; cuffs, edges of sleeves and hems were all protected with decorative symbols. As man moved further away from these original intentions he became more superstitious and embroidery was placed along the seams, on the tops of stockings, knitted into socks, bound around the head on braid or material and used on veils and hats. Today these features are still evident, for example, in Lapland where the colours and designs have kept their simplicity: when embroidery was not used the edge of the garment was left fringed, later followed by lace.

One of the oldest of man's symbols has been the circle and interlocking spiral, which can be traced from the Stone Age and ancient China. It appears in Celtic patterns, as well as maori tattoos and Islamic arabesques. The circle represented perfection, completeness, unity and the Creator. The spiral or labyrinth design represents man's rebirth into life and the path from the world towards the divine.

Apart from the circle and labyrinth, there was the triangle, an ancient symbol with cosmic and religious significance. Throughout the years these symbols became embellished with many decorative patterns. Many of the old designs can still be seen, but others have changed completely. The circle became a sun, wheel or flower, the spiral became a serpent, triangles became stars and the 'Tree of Life' carried many motifs.

With the passing of the years, stitchcraft took on powerful meanings: there was a significance in whether the stitches passed from left to right or east to west. The cross, used both in stitching and design, represented the four cardinal points of the world with the fifth point being the vertical direction arising from the centre. Known as the cosmic quadrangle, it was an important symbol of life.

Each country developed its own individual designs and within a country each region, village and valley had variations. Many of the old designs have been preserved as families have passed them down from generation to generation, but other patterns have changed with the passing of time. Patterns began to reflect environment and were incorporated into the older designs. Embroidery and costume became a form of identity revealing country, region and even village and trade.

Symbols are closely linked to the great religions of the world and the religious factor had a great influence on designs:

Islamic religion forbade the reproduction of living creatures and so a very elaborate form of patterns developed. Stylized animals appeared in many countries and scorpions and spiders were used as warning symbols.

Colours played an important part in costume and embroidery. Dyes such as yellow came from saffron, the stamen of the crocus, vine leaves and the rinds of pomegranates. Red came from madder together with kermes, or cochineal, an insect found in the kermes oak or in cacti; blue came from the indigo plant. The roots, stalks, seeds and fruits were all utilized in many ingenious ways. The depth of colour was controlled by the type of water used – for example, rain, river or spring. The time of the year in which the plant was harvested also affected the colour, as did the quality of the soil. Vegetable dyes proved to have a richer and more natural colour, but these became lost with the introduction of aniline and other chemical dyes.

Colours came to have different meanings in different countries: for example, in Europe and America black denotes mourning, but in China white is associated with grief. The Syrians and Armenians wear light blue for mourning, in the Far East yellow is used and in Iran the colour is that of withered leaves.

Red is a very popular colour as it expressed happiness, life and love, and it is also worn as a protective charm: many necklaces are made of red beads or coral. In Italy and Sicily pieces of coral tied around the neck with red braid were worn by children and the necklace was called a *bulla* by the Romans.

In other countries blue beads are worn for the same reason. Metal was also supposed to have special powers and small mirrors and sequins were incorporated into patterns to ward off evil spirits. Metal thread was used for the same reason. Metal was also considered to contain very special powers and necklaces, earrings, bracelets, rings, clasps on belts and the circling of metal belts had the same properties and intentions as embroidery. Stones were also believed to possess magic powers and were made into necklaces and sewn onto costumes. They were passed from generation to generation and were symbols of the self being complete, unchanging and lasting.

## THE HAT

In many civilizations the head was considered to be the seat of power as well as the highest point of man's body. Many religious traditions, legends and rituals have developed round this idea. This very sensitive and vulnerable part of the body has always required some form of protection. The hat developed with a threefold purpose: it offered protection from the elements, it became a sign of status and it was used for rituals.

Early man used animal skins incorporating these three ideas. The skins not only provided covering for the body and the head, but it was believed that from these a vital force could be inherited and that this power would enable the wearers to become more efficient as hunters and gain control over animals.

The horns and other parts of the animal were used as decoration. A hat made of skin is still worn by those who depend upon hunting for their livelihood.

In many countries shepherds still wear sheepskin hats and jackets, and the hats range from neat round ones to the large shaggy types, as well as knitted woollen caps. The wearing of animal heads at carnivals stems from these old traditions.

The feathers of birds were also used extensively for head-dresses. The feathers of the eagle were very popular in many countries where this bird was greatly revered and looked upon as a symbol of power and strength. Native North Americans also used them to denote rank and bravery as well as power. During their ceremonies, plumes symbolized the carrying of prayers upwards in the same way as lighted candles do in religious ceremonies.

Various tribes in Africa and South America, as well as those in the Pacific, have beautiful head-dresses made entirely of feathers, and are so designed to give a halo effect, thus glorifying the head. In Europe feathers are sometimes worn on the side of a hat.

Tree worship was expressed by the use of foliage in the making of a head-dress. Floral crowns and wreaths show the links associated with the various deities of the earth and of fertility. Flowers had special meanings, as with the use of colours, and they were carefully blended according to the season of the year or the occasion. Many floral head-dresses are still worn but others have been replaced by floral posies which can be used on either men's or women's hats.

Hats were linked with the creation by the people of Asia in the making of hats with plaited straw or rushes. These give protection from both the sun and rain and can be seen in China, Japan and the Far East, and the shape has only changed slightly throughout the years.

As man developed and tribes gradually migrated to other environments, the use of fur was not always practical and this led to the making of felt through the matting of fur. This material is thought to be one of the oldest invented, even preceding the weaving of wool and cotton.

The first type of hat in Europe was probably round, fitting well onto the head like a skullcap and made of felt. In Greece and Rome this was known as a *petasus* or *pileus* and is still worn in the Arab States. The skullcap also represented liberty and when a Roman slave obtained his freedom, his head was shaved and he was allowed to wear the *pileus*. The skullcap was also worn by the Celts. Gradually a shallow brim was added to the crown and the hat became similar to that depicted worn by Mercury and Hermes. The brim was for added protection against the sun. The hat began to be linked with position or trade and a type of cap was evolved for seafaring men: Ulysses is often shown wearing one of these.

From Persia came the Phrygian bonnet, a hat which originated in Asia Minor and the East, and which became the basis of many styles. Originally it was worn by the Persian soldiers and was a short, pointed, conical-shaped hat much favoured by the god Mithras. His religious influence brought it to England and might well have been responsible for the appearance of the Saxon type of hat with which it had much in common.

The hats of peasants stayed simple and were adapted for their work or trade. Many countries had strict sumptuary laws that clearly defined what they could and could not wear. When these laws began to be repealed the women copied some of the court styles.

Christianity had demanded codes of dress and uncovered heads for women, particularly in church, were forbidden. They were expected to wear a wimple at all times and this is reflected in the general use of headscarves. The covering of the head became an essential part of peasant costume and different types of head covering for married or unmarried women were evolved.

In the fifteenth and sixteenth centuries in France and the Flemish countries, the relaxing of the laws regulating costume coincided with the growth of the lace-making industry. Hats and head-dresses appeared made of starched cotton and lace. Many of these were not practicable for work, but were worn on Sundays. It was during this period that many new head-dresses were designed.

Climate also played its part in the shaping of a hat. In the colder countries sheepskin and other fur was generally used: in Tibet, earflaps were devised, a style also found in other countries.

In hot climates, hats with wide brims were necessary and the horsemen of North and South America, Mexico, Spain and the Hungarian Plains all wore hats with wide brims.

Straw hats in various shapes and sizes were found from the Far East to the Americas and were worn both by men and women. In Portugal a small felt hat is worn by the women which gives shade to the eyes, but no protection to the neck. A headscarf is draped over the head and then

the hat placed on top: this style is also found in the Canary Islands. In Italy the women wear draped and folded material to protect their heads and in other countries there are capes, mantillas or wimples for head wear. In countries where the women carry large water jars or baskets on their heads, they have flat pads (sometimes known as mother-in-laws).

Countries which came under the Ottoman Empire adopted the Turkish custom of veiling, and veils are worn in many of the Balkan countries. Turbans, fez or the draped *kaffiyeh* are worn by men of the Islamic faith and these have a religious significance as well as acting as a protection against the weather. Turbans are a protection against the sands of the desert and the Tuareg men of the southern Sahara wear turbans with veils, similar in type to the turban style of hat worn by the women of Fano, Denmark. This hat has a mask that covers the lower half of the face and acts as a protection against the sand whipped up from the dunes. In parts of the former Yugoslavia and Albania the men wear a turban which also wraps around the neck and this is a protection against the cold in winter and the heat in summer.

Many factors have gone into the shaping of hats and head-dresses; for example, the discarded hats of Napoleon's army in retreat influenced those in Austria. Another example is the wearing of a baby's christening robe on the head, as is found in Mexico.

The hat or head-dress also denoted rank: that worn by the head of a tribe differed from the rest. Head coverings and colours also changed within the different regions of a country: special hats were used for funerals, festive occasions, Sundays, winter and summer. There was a marked difference between the hats of married and unmarried women, as well as between village and village or tribes.

## SHOES

In comparison with other items of clothing, shoes have changed very little over the years. In social circles shoes went through every conceivable style and shape, although these changes did not affect the rural worker. For the land, a tougher and long-lasting shoe was essential; once this was established it remained unaffected by fashion. Shoes were expensive to buy and were not easily made in the home. Unlike other articles of clothing which could be woven and stitched together shoes required the instruments of the shoemaker's craft. Peasants found a simple design that was economical and practical.

Early settlers wore no shoes and for many this is still ideal and a solution to the problem. In some countries it is not unusual to find country people walking for miles barefooted and putting on shoes just before they enter a town.

A very early Egyptian drawing depicts a nobleman walking barefooted followed by a servant carrying his shoes in readiness for when they would be required. At one time shoes were a status symbol and peasants and slaves were not encouraged to emulate their masters. It was also considered effeminate for men in some countries to wear sandals. Slaves were often kept shoeless in order to prevent escape.

One of the earliest forms of shoe or sandal was probably made from woven palm leaves, papyrus or vegetable fibre. The design was very simple and the shoe was kept in place by bands of linen or leather thongs. Various names were given to the earlier form of shoe, one being the Latin *solea* from which comes the English word sole. The rope-soled, canvas-topped *alpargatas* of Spain, the espadrilles of France, the *ciocie* of Italy (from the Latin *sicyonia*) and the *ushutas* of South America all have their origins in the simple type of shoe produced by the Roman civilization.

Another type of peasant sandal that has survived through the centuries is the flat sole, which is kept in place by two straps. This form of footwear has its present day counterpart in the Japanese *geta* or *zori* and the sandals of Arabia, North Africa and parts of South America. The early Greek actors and comedians wore a light pull-on shoe or slipper called a *soccus*, from which comes the word sock. Eventually the *soccus*, which was made from soft leather or wool, had a division between the first and second toes and was worn by the more privileged person and was another form of flat sandal. It was the forerunner of the Japanese *tabi* or *jak tabi*, the worker's shoe.

One of the basic peasant shoes was made from animal skin and a piece of leather was bound to the foot with cross thonging. Sometimes the lacing was tied around the ankle or it was criss-crossed around the lower leg or trouser. There are numerous examples of this type of shoe to be found, from that of the Scottish ghillie, the mountaineer's shoe from Poland to those of the Balkan countries. In many of these shoes a pronounced turned-up shoe is found and this developed from the thonging of the leather which caused the end to curl slightly upwards. It was also a protection for the toes against rough ground or stones.

In early days the use of animal skins for shoes followed the same superstitious belief associated with the use of skins for clothing – that the speed, courage and strength of the dead animal would be transmitted to the wearer. A form of moccasin was worn by native North Americans and these varied according to the climate. Those who settled in the Arctic regions wrapped sealskin around the legs and a type of fur boot evolved. This is also found with the Lapps in Greenland and those living in Siberia. The fur is often worn inside for greater warmth, as with slippers. In warmer regions, the fur was removed and only the skin used.

Wood is a material that was not often used for footwear although occasionally a sole was made from it. Lacking pliability, wood restricted the foot's movement.

Wooden soles were once strapped to the feet of Roman prisoners, making any form of escape difficult. The wooden sabot or clog developed from the high wooden pattens worn by ladies of fashion to protect their shoes from the muddy streets of the sixteenth, seventeenth and eighteenth centuries. The peasants wore a patten called a *galoche*, which originated in the Ardennes and which had wooden soles, but leather tops. The wooden shoe proved to be serviceable and popular in the Low Countries and France, as they kept the feet dry and were hardwearing. They were made from willow, poplar or any strong wood which did not split. They were generally used in flat countries: mountain people required a shoe that enabled them to grip a rough surface.

A clog-makers guild was formed in the Netherlands in 1570 and this type of footwear is still used in some areas of the country to the present day. It did not appear in England until a much later date and became popular with the millworkers in the north during the nineteenth century. Clogs and sabots are essentially work shoes and were replaced on Sundays or other festive occasions with leather shoes, often with a silver buckle and in a style copied from those of the eighteenth century.

The other form of peasant footwear was the boot and this developed to give necessary protection round the calf and ankle. Thorns, animal bites and the chafing of horse-riding, as well as cold weather and snow called for the protection of the lower leg by using skins, leather, and bark of trees, cloth, metal coverings and even rings. In time the leggings became attached to the shoe, although there was always the alternative of using them separately.

The boot was known in ancient civilizations and was particularly popular among soldiers, with red as a predominant colour as it absorbed the bloodstains from the toes, a result of arduous training. With the development of military uniforms, this colour was replaced by black. The popularity of the boot was carried through Europe by a succession of invading armies and, in particular, by the skilled horsemen. Cowboys and other horsemen adopted the boot as essential wear and in countries such as Poland, Hungary and Russia, with their military and equine backgrounds, it was worn by the peasantry.

# ICELAND

ICELAND, A COUNTRY OF waterfalls, volcanoes, green valleys and hot geysers, has gained fame for its literature, especially the sagas and skaldic poetry which developed and flourished in the thirteenth century. The main folk activity has always been song rather than dance, with its close link to the literary background; another reason is that the island lacks trees or the natural materials for making musical instruments to provide a background for dancing.

Apart from the main industry of fishing, Iceland has over two million sheep. Thus wool is naturally used extensively for clothing, being both warm and protective. Unlike other northern peoples, who favour light colours, the Icelanders have the proclivity for using black; this may be because they do not have natural resources for making dyes.

Older women wear long, full, black skirts with a black bodice and sleeves. The bodice is either laced up with gold cord or with two gold buttons and a gold brooch, and it is decorated with gold and green embroidery. Patterns circle the skirt at about calf height and decorate the hem. Designs are usually of leaves and the curving motif shows the Celtic background combined with the Viking love of gold.

A white or coloured blouse is worn under the bodice and a gold linked chain belt worn at the waist. Some of the younger girls wear sleeveless bodices, black skirts and a full apron of blue or checked material.

Head-dresses are unusual and very original in design. A gold band fits around a small white hat with a curled crown, rather like the Phrygian-style hat, and over this a fine white veil is draped. The hair is often dressed in two plaits that are looped up and caught at the back or left to hang down either side. A firm leather shoe is worn.

*Icelandic hat.*

ICELAND. *The woman on the left wears the more elaborate costume used on ceremonial occasions. The unusual head-dress is an old style now rarely seen. The hat of the woman on the right is more typical. The bunch of keys hanging from her belt indicates that she is married. The other woman wears a typical everyday costume.*

*The black velvet skullcap has a long black tassel on the right side that is fixed to the cap with gold rings. The man wears black breeches, a high-cut waistcoat and a jacket which has many silver buttons. Leather gaiters are worn over stout shoes and a woollen skullcap provides protection against the weather.*

# LAPLAND

LAPLAND IS THE HOME OF THE LAPPS, or Samek as they prefer to be called. These nomadic people, who follow the reindeer herds, have a highly developed culture, adapted to their way of life and the hardship of living in sub-zero temperatures.

Lapland is an area that stretches across the top of Norway, Sweden and Finland. The Lapps are known as Finnish Lapps or named after the country in which they reside. Although they share the same background and culture they are an independent and separate people. The whole of their life centres around the reindeer, which is used for food, clothing, trading and transport, the animals being harnessed to sledges; even the gut is used for sewing skins together.

Their costumes, like their way of life, have hardly altered over the years. In winter both sexes wear tunics and trousers made from reindeer skins, usually with the hair worn inside for added warmth. Underneath the outer garments are woollen shirts and jumpers to give further protection. Reindeer-skin boots are worn in the winter; the insides are often padded with a type of rush grass that helps to keep the feet warm. In the summer the fur tunics and trousers are exchanged for a similar type of garment made of wool and usually blue in colour, and moccasins with a slightly turned-up toe are worn.

Red and yellow patterned braid is used for decoration and this is placed around the neck, down the front, on all the seams and around the hem of the tunic. The use of braid follows the old custom of warding off evil spirits.

It is interesting to note that, because of their isolation, the Lapp costume is a perfect example of the type of basic garment worn by most races in Europe. The remoteness of the country has not exposed its inhabitants to the fashionable influences of other countries.

There are several variations of headdress, which differ according to the area. Because of the cold climate the men stuff their 'cap of the four winds' with down or reindeer hair. It is always important to keep the top of the head warm.

Both men and women wear a tunic, but that of the woman is slightly longer and she wears a red woollen bonnet.

Over their tunics they wear a wide leather belt studded with silver ornaments and fastened with a silver clasp. A knife is usually fixed into the belt, an essential piece of equipment for the Lapp. Both sexes wear thick mittens and there is an old tradition that when a man wished to court a girl he would try and pull a mitten off her hand, which she allowed if she agreed. The illustration shows the different styles of costume found in Lapland.

LAPLAND. *The man wears a light-coloured tunic and trousers, although these are frequently in a bright blue similar to those worn by the little boy. The cap is old in origin and not always worn today. Thanks to the four points on the crown, it came to be known as the 'cap of the four winds'. Originally the cap had a square crown but the four corners were gradually pulled out, making it into four points. A knot of coloured ribbons is fixed to the head-band. If the man places all the points of his cap forward they denote that he is unmarried. The woman is wearing a traditional summer costume. The little bonnet is edged with lace and she wears a brightly coloured apron and shawl. The boy wears a typical costume and a tight, warm cap which has a large red pompom on top. All the shoes are made from reindeer skin.*

# FINLAND

FINLAND, OR SUOMI as it is called in Finnish, is bounded on the west by Sweden and on the east by Russia. Over the past 800 years the country has been ruled by Denmark, Sweden and Russia, but the Swedish influence has been the greatest as their sovereignty lasted over 600 years. It was only in 1917 that Finland became an independent State. Possibly because of their long history of occupation, the Finns have developed a reserved approach to life and to other people and this quality is reflected in their dances and costumes, which reflect an inherent dignity.

As in most northern countries, Midsummer's Eve is celebrated with bonfires, music and dancing and is an event not to be missed after the long, dark and cold winter. The value attached to the summer months is shown in the use of colours for their costumes: yellows, blues, reds, greens and white . . . all of which reflect the sun, summer skies, flowers, grass and the forests and lakes for which Finland is famed.

The costumes are simple, but very attractive, often made of vertically striped material. Skirts are fairly long and are heavy, suitable for a country with such a rigorous climate demanding added protection against the cold. Bodices and skirts made of the same striped material are very popular, and there are variations in their wear, such as a striped bodice with plain skirt or vice versa. The bodices, which are always sleeveless, can be laced up the front, fastened with two, three or four silver buttons, caught with a silver clasp or crossed over and fastened with two rows of buttons. A white apron is sometimes worn, either plain or embroidered, and a white blouse with long full sleeves and a high neck ending in a little frill, a round edge or a small collar. A loose pocket, similar to those of Sweden and Norway and showing individual variations in embroidery, is fastened at the waist. A round silver brooch of traditional design, often reflecting sun worship and a legacy from the Viking and Nordic races, is pinned on to the blouse or, alternatively, a silver chain necklace is worn. Jewellery is passed down through the generations and the men's silver or brass buttons also pass from generation to generation.

The head-dress consists of a little cap edged with lace and with a bow fixed at the back. In some areas these bows have long ends. Young girls tie a ribbon around their hair and let the long ribbon ends hang down the back. White or red stockings are usually worn with silver-buckled black shoes. Cotton has been used for many items of clothing since the nineteenth century, when a Scotsman, James Finlayson, started a cotton mill in Tampere.

The men's costumes, which show more Swedish influence than those of the

# FINLAND

FINLAND. The two women wear different styles of bodices. The woman wearing the red bodice comes from the west of Finland. The two buttons that are undone on her bodice denote that she is married and her lace-edged bonnet is also an indication of her married status. The girl in green wears a costume from the south-west. Young girls and unmarried women wear a ribbon in their hair with the long ends flowing down the back. The costume of the man on the right is from Askola, near Helsinki. His waistcoat and breeches show a very strong Swedish influence. The man on the left, carrying the large black felt hat, wears an older-style costume from Kaukola. His moccasin-type shoe is like those worn in the summer by the Lapps.

women, are sober – black or dark blue breeches or trousers, with a jacket to match, worn with a double-breasted waistcoat, striped and fastened with two rows of silver or brass buttons. The shirt is white with a stand-up collar, fastened at the neck with a silver brooch. White or dark red socks are worn and either a skull cap or a felt hat. Black shoes with silver buckles are most commonly used.

# NORWAY

ALTHOUGH SCANDINAVIAN countries share much in common, each country has developed its own folklore, costumes and dances. In spite of hundreds of years of domination, only achieving full independence in 1905, the Norwegians have preserved their own traditions. Midsummer Day is celebrated all over the country with bonfires and replaces the old pagan festival held in honour of the sun, or *solsnu*. There are many customs and stories relating to trolls, giants, mermen, mermaids and water spirits.

The costumes throughout Norway are extremely attractive, with many marked differences from those of neighbouring countries. The difficult terrain, of mountains, fjords and forests, together with the climate, has kept travel to a minimum within the country and has led to a very individual development of costume in each area. Through the long dark winters, materials were woven and dyed, garments embroidered and stockings knitted. Old Viking patterns were used, but the embroidery on the bodice or skirt hem reveals the wearer's region. The designs are often geometrical with shapes reminiscent of enlarged snow crystals.

The length of the women's skirts varies from long, calf or ankle length to the fairly short double skirt of Setesdal. The skirts allow dancers to move freely and steps are executed with a lilting quality. The costume from Setesdal has a double flared skirt with stiffened bands of red and green at the hem, which make the skirt stand out. In Hallingdal, a valley north-west of Oslo, the women's skirts have a medieval line, the fullness coming from a very high-cut bodice with no waistline. A white long-sleeved blouse is worn with most costumes and this is caught at the neck with a silver brooch. Beaten silver and gold jewellery is worn a great deal and again the designs reflect Viking ancestry. In western Telemark, on her wedding day, a girl is given a large brooch, usually an heirloom, representing the sun.

NORWAY. *The couple on the right wear the very popular costume from Voss. The women's red bodice is embroidered with tiny white and coloured beads, also repeated on the sides of the bonnet. The white apron shows intricate drawn-thread work. Unmarried women and young girls from this region wear either a little red bonnet tied under the chin with a red ribbon or are bareheaded. Married women wear a specially folded white headscarf. Stockings are usually black, although white is popular with children.*

*Silver-buckled black shoes are worn. The girl on the left is wearing a costume from east Telemark. The man from Voss wears a typical Norwegian costume of a waistcoat and breeches; sometimes a black jacket and silver buttons is also worn. The man from Telemark wears a particularly striking costume all in black and white, relieved only by silver buttons. The stand-up coat collar shows the influence of the eighteenth century, while his white stockings are knitted according to a special pattern.*

Unlike Denmark and Sweden, where the bodices are mostly plain, Norway favours bodices embroidered on the sides, around the edges or on a central panel. The motif, especially in the central and eastern areas, is of baroque acanthus leaves worked in coloured wools.

On the west coast many of the costumes have loose pockets or bags, attached to the belts by silver hooks. Head-dresses are simple, married women usually tucking their hair away, unmarried women wearing little caps or bonnets which are tied under the chin or, alternatively just a band around the head.

The men wear black breeches tied below the knees with coloured braid.

Waistcoats can be black, red or green and are fastened with a double row of silver or brass buttons. Short jackets are worn, which are decorated with buttons and form an important part of the man's costume in many regions. An unusual costume comes from Setesdal, where the men wear a type of dungaree with a short jacket embroidered in red, yellow and green.

It is thought that in the past many Norwegian men became mercenary soldiers and brought back other ideas from abroad; for example, the leather on the trousers in the Setesdal costume is thought to be based on the pattern of the uniform of the Spanish cavalry.

# SWEDEN

SWEDEN IS THE LARGEST OF the Scandinavian countries and in common with her neighbours, Norway and Denmark, her early history follows a similar pattern of Viking domination. Festivals are held to celebrate the light and sun, one of the most popular being Midsummer Eve. Maypoles are decorated with green branches and flowers, and dancing continues through a night which has no darkness, being so far north. In the province Dalarna, 'the heart of Sweden', this festival is particularly colourful, with everyone wearing national costume and dancing traditional dances. The other important festival is that on Walpurgis Eve, 30 April, when bonfires are lit to celebrate the advent of spring following the long dark days of winter.

Swedish costumes are simpler in style than those of Denmark. The skirts are not as long or as heavy, allowing for greater freedom of movement, as well as precision in the dance steps. They are usually plain in colour, either blue, red, green, yellow or black, chosen to reflect the colours of the countryside as well as the seasons.

The bodice or corselet is usually laced

SWEDEN. *All these costumes come from the area around Stockholm. Both the women wear simple little bonnets, one in red and the other in white. The brightly coloured shawls are a feature of this area, and are fastened with silver filigree brooches. The loose pocket serves as a type of bag, and the embroidery on the bag reflects the parish of the wearer. In some regions of Sweden a band around the bottom of the skirt signified that the wearer was single; two bands indicated that she was married. Both the men wear breeches; the yellow pair are frequently made of a soft leather whereas the dark blue would be in cloth. The waistcoats and trousers are fastened with silver buttons. A very popular feature are the red pompoms that are worn below the knee and, in some costumes, on the laces of the shoes. Some women's bonnets would also have two red pompoms at the back. The black shoes with silver buckles are typical of Scandinavia.*

up at the front and worn over a white long-sleeved blouse. The lacing on the bodice passes through eyelets made of silver or pewter.

Each region has its own type of apron or costume. Aprons can be either plain, with perpendicular stripes, horizontal stripes or plain with horizontal stripes at the bottom only; alternatively, they can be flowered, checked or plain white. In Stockholm, blue is worn, a colour which is very popular in Sweden, and also used extensively in Finland and Lapland. Newly married women or newcomers to a parish are expected to conform to the costume of that village.

The head-dress is fairly simple, consisting of various kinds of bonnets or caps which turn up at the back. In some areas unmarried girls wear red bonnets and the married women wear white. Married women are not expected to show their hair, so it is tucked away into the bonnet, or a cap.

Shawls are worn with many of the costumes and in Stockholm these are bright red, patterned with flowers with a red-fringed edge. The shawl is worn rather like a cape, fastened in front with a brooch. In Värmland the shawl is white, decorated on the edge with a red design and is similar to a large white collar. The girls in Östergötland wear a similar shawl, but tuck the front ends into the waistband.

*A Swedish pocket.*

At Leksand, in Dalarna, the shawl is white, patterned with red roses, and the same material is used to make a tight-fitting bonnet.

Many costumes have braided belts ending with bright tassels. The problem of having no pockets is resolved by the wearing of a type of reticule or *aumônière*. This is a flat bag, either square or oval in shape and embroidered with bright-coloured wools; it is suspended from the waistband by a coloured braid, usually from the left hip. This type of pocket or pouch has been in use since Greek and Roman times. Red stockings are usually worn with black shoes.

The man's costume is similar to those found in other Scandinavian countries; yellow or dark blue breeches fastened below the knee with red braid and pompoms. The waistcoat can be red or striped and is fastened down the front with metal buttons. A white shirt, white or blue stockings and black shoes with brass or silver buckles complete the costume. A type of skullcap in red, blue or black and decorated with red, yellow or black braid, or in some regions a top hat or a woollen Phrygian-style cap is worn.

# DENMARK

DENMARK IS THE SMALLEST of the Scandinavian countries, but at one time it was the most powerful and was the cultural centre of the Nordic race. The Reformation in Scandinavia, however, had a sobering effect, both on costume and dance. Many of the old dances lapsed and peasant dress became very conservative.

Costumes are still worn on some of the islands and in coastal areas by the fisherfolk. Women favour rather long and somewhat heavy skirts, either gathered or pleated; the skirt is full, allowing plenty of room for movement, but length and weight gives a heavy quality to dancing.

Peasants usually wove their own materials from wool and used simple designs. Affluent farmers' wives and townspeople would, on special occasions, wear silk which often had accordion pleats. The dress from Amager, originally used for church-going, has a red pleated skirt edged with a black border. Pleats were formed by hand – first the skirt was dampened, then the pleats were pressed in, and the skirt was wrapped in a muslin cloth and put in an oven to dry. This process was known as 'cooked' pleating.

The most popular colours are green, red and yellow, representing the colours of the landscape and seasons. Many costumes have bodices and skirts of the same colour and material, but there are many variations, such as red stripes on a dark background worn with a blue bodice, or fine yellow stripes on red worn with a red top. Colour also reveals marital status: in Fano, red skirts are worn by married and older women and myrtle green by the young ones.

An unusual feature is for the sleeveless bodice to be worn over a blouse or dress of contrasting colour. A costume from Mols shows a dark blue bodice worn with long red sleeves: a similar costume from the Praestoe area has a red and green striped bodice edged with green and worn with red three-quarter-length sleeves.

Large aprons, reaching nearly to the hem of the skirt, are found in most areas. Some are so large they resemble a skirt. A check pattern is very popular; the checks can be large or small and vary in colour. A costume worn in Roemeo shows green and yellow checks on a dark background and worn over a red skirt. White aprons with a drawn-thread design, embroidered in white or patterned, are also popular; the aprons are made of cotton, but silk is used for special occasions.

The head-dress is based on a simple form of bonnet, often in a plain material; married women wear black or dark colours and young girls wear

*A masked head-dress from Fano.*

DENMARK. *The young woman in red on the left wears a country-style dress from Odense, the birthplace of Hans Christian Andersen. A feature of Danish costumes are the many different bonnets. From the shape it was possible to tell which the region, village, marital and social status of the wearer or that she was in mourning. The woman from Odense wears a white lace bonnet with a red over-bonnet decorated with gold embroidery. On the back is a blue silk bow. Although this rather Puritan style covers the hair, the use of white shows that she is unmarried. The more elaborate dark costume on the right comes from Falster, near the border with Germany in the east. This costume is worn by married women, the material being darker and the bonnet covering the face. This costume would be used for special occasions such as attending church on Sundays. The man comes from the coastal area in east Jutland and wears the typical yellow breeches seen in Denmark and Sweden. This is a working costume, so the buttons are plain rather than silver. Many men wear a sleeveless waistcoat over a white shirt. The red woollen fisherman's hat is found in many regions and is common to seafaring men in many parts of Europe. The heavy black shoes are worn with or without silver buckles, which are for special occasions.*

white. In the Medebo region, a coloured scarf is tied over the bonnet. At Fano, on the north sea coast, a curious mask is worn as a protection against the sand whipped up by the gales.

Small check-patterned shawls are sometimes worn. Red checks on a navy background are a sign of joy, but blue or green checks on navy are a recognized sign of mourning.

The men wear breeches caught below the knees with bands and tassels; colours are yellow, white or black, according to the district. Striped waistcoats decorated with silver buttons are worn and if a man wears a yellow silk waistcoat, it signifies that he has crossed the equator. A jacket can be worn with this waistcoat, likewise decorated with silver buttons. Under the waistcoat is worn a white shirt with a stand-up collar around which is knotted a colourful handkerchief. A red stocking cap with a tassel is popular as headgear. Both sexes wear black shoes with silver buckles.

# THE NETHERLANDS

THE NATIONAL CHARACTER of the Dutch people is reflected in their costumes, which show considerable differences between regions and even villages. Many are still worn while others only appear at festival times or on special occasions. A costume can reveal the religion and marital status of the wearer, social position and whether from an agricultural or fishing background; it can also show mourning.

The skirts are usually made of heavy home-spun black wool, under which several heavy petticoats are worn to keep out the cold. Red was at one time the most popular colour for the petticoats. The skirts are full, allowing for freedom of movement when working outdoors. There is a great contrast between the sombre clothes worn for work and the garments worn on Sundays or festive occasions. In some regions costumes change from winter to summer when lighter skirts are worn. Striped material is very popular and is used for aprons and skirts. Aprons can be plain, as in the fishing village of Scheveningen, where black silk is worn for Sundays and blue cotton for weekdays.

In Staphorst aprons are black with an upper border of pink or white check material. Other regions reverse the designs, having a check lower section and a plain-coloured border, or the apron is checked with no border.

There are several types of bodices, which are usually sleeveless and cut with a

THE NETHERLANDS. *The couple both wear costumes from the fishing village of Volendam in the north. The woman wears a costume for Sunday wear, shown by the black apron with the decorated floral band at the top. On weekdays the apron would be striped. The costume consists of a 'tight wrap' made in the same material as the floral band of the apron. Worn over this is a tight-fitting over-bodice or jacket, which has a braided square neckline. Volendam women wear short hair which they tuck into a little black cap. On top of the cap is placed the lace-winged bonnet. For mourning the 'tight wrap', the band on the apron and the beads would be black. At one time the skirt was also black but a more colourful skirt is now worn. The man wears the black, baggy seaman's trousers, fastened in the front with silver buttons. These type of trousers are a relic of an earlier age, when fishermen generally wore them. The trousers are tied at the back with a green cord, or black for mourning. The shirt collar is embroidered in black cross stitch and fastened with two gold studs. Over the shirt a striped waistcoat and black jacket are worn. In his fisherman's cap he wears three green ribbons at the back; one would indicate that he was engaged, but three mean that he is married.*

*A 'tight wrap' from Spakenburg.*

round high neck. Known as a 'tight wrap', they are worn over a vest with long or elbow-length sleeves. In Marken the tight wrap has a flowered pattern using embroidered coloured wools: two roses from the age of six to sixteen, and fastened at the back; from sixteen onwards, five roses and a front fastening; and for a bride there are seven roses. The undervest or sleeves are of red and white stripes. In some areas a jacket is worn over the tight wrap, either buttoned to the neck or with an open neckline. Shawls are of lace, wool, silk or a checked material, of various sizes, and are worn in a variety of ways. The Burghers' costume from Friesland is particularly attractive – the dresses are made of patterned silk with a white lace fichu or shawl and apron, together with a châtelaine bag hanging from a belt.

One of the most interesting aspects of the women's costumes are the numerous head-caps. The custom of wearing a cap developed from the days when they were worn in the house. The caps vary from two or three separate sections up to twelve; they are worn over a type of head-clip or head-band that holds and supports the complicated lace and pleated material. The bands are made of gold and usually end in an ornament. Gold pins fasten the band to the cap and these can also end in square, oval or spiral shapes. Sometimes the metal decoration protrudes from under the cap and lies on the forehead or flat against the cheeks. Round discs signify the Catholic religion, squares denote Protestants. Two, three or four rows of coral beads, fastening

with a gold clip at the front or back, are worn with most costumes. Coral is regarded as lucky. Black stockings are worn with most costumes, apart from those of the Burghers from Friesland where white stockings are worn.

Men's costumes are far less complicated. Fishermen wear wide, black, baggy trousers, the fullness allowing plenty of freedom for working on the boats. These trousers are modelled on those worn by seventeenth-century seamen. The men of Urk wear wide trousers which end just below the knee and are similar to knickerbockers, or the *bragou-braz* of the Breton sailors.

A similar type of trouser is worn on the island of Marken, but they are slightly shorter and are white in summer and black in winter: black stockings are worn. Fishermen wear either a shaggy cap or sometimes a hat; farmers are distinguished by less baggy trousers and by a peaked cap. Trousers are usually fastened in front with a flap and two buttons, often made of silver. Long-sleeved, double-breasted and collarless jackets, fastening up to the neck with two rows of silver buttons, are worn in many areas. In Staphorst the working jacket is dark blue and tucked into the trousers, with white braces over the top.

Shirts are long-sleeved and fastened at the neck with two silver or gold collar studs. Blue and white stripes are popular, especially for weekdays, with a change to black or a dark colour for Sundays. A knotted tie is worn under the front studs and the colour can denote mourning, with black and white for half-mourning. At one time a silver watch and chain were worn; if the chain was worn horizontally it conveyed that the wearer was married, but if left to dangle it signified a bachelor.

In Marken boys and girls are dressed alike in skirts up to the age of six, but small details denote the sex of the child. The boys have studs in their collars and horizontal slit pockets in their skirts, whereas the girls have vertical pockets. There are also slight changes in the colours and patterns.

Clogs are worn by both sexes for every-day wear and work. In Marken they are varnished black with a coloured pattern and bear the wearer's initials. At one time in Scheveningen the clogs were sandpaper-white, while in other areas they were painted, decorated and carved. It was a custom for young men to present clogs that they had carved and decorated to their fiancées. For Sundays, black shoes with silver buckles are worn.

# FRANCE

FRANCE IS ONE OF THE LARGEST countries in Europe, stretching from the English Channel in the north to the Mediterranean in the south. In the west is the long coastline that borders the Atlantic Ocean, and France has boundaries with Spain, Italy, Switzerland, Germany, Luxembourg and Belgium. French costumes, like the music and dances, are neat and simple in style. In a country as large and diverse as France, there are numerous variations, with each costume showing an individuality and a practical style devoid of any overelaboration.

Women's skirts are full, but not voluminous or pleated, thus allowing plenty of room for movement. Material can be a plain colour, floral, patterned, striped or have one or two broad bands around the

hem when the skirt is plain. In Normandy the whole dress is made in royal blue, green or deep purple. In Alsace the skirt is red with bands of black velvet ribbon around the hem. In Champagne the skirts are made of dark blue, or of dark-orange silk or cotton. Striped cotton skirts in pink, green and blue on a white background are worn by those working in the vineyards of Burgundy. Aprons also vary; they may be white, coloured, or made or edged with lace. Many of the costumes are accompanied by delightful shawls or fichus; some are made or trimmed with lace, others are of a plain or patterned material, and several have a fringed edge. Bodices are usually laced up the front and are worn with either long- or short-sleeved blouses. The bodice was thought to have evolved from one which was worn by Queen Marie

FRANCE. This couple come from Brittany in the north-west part of France. The woman is wearing a costume from Pont Aven. It is worn at weddings, one of the local pardons or for church on Sunday. The bodice is trimmed with velvet, braid and lace with a lace 'modesty vest' worn across the front opening. A large goffered collar is made of fine linen or muslin and is edged with lace; a special goffering iron is used to make the material fluted and stiff. The full skirt of satin or silk has a deep border of embroidered velvet. The head-dress or coif is made of stiffened lace and the two wings are fixed onto a little cap covered with blue ribbon. The ribbon is knotted into a bow to secure the ends of the lace. There are several variations of this costume. The man is from Quimper in Finistère and is wearing a dark-navy jacket and trousers in a lighter shade of blue. The design on the jacket is in gold braid with a Celtic design of curling leaves. The black felt hat with a round crown has a brim with a rolling edge. A velvet ribbon is caught at the back with a silver buckle. At one time hand-carved and decorated sabots were worn but are now rarely seen.

of Anjou in the fifteenth century.

The main feature of French costumes are the women's hats and head-dresses, of which there are hundreds of different styles. Each region or village has its own particular design. In Normandy, the head-dress is very tall and called a *bourgoins*. Made of starched muslin, fine linen and lace, it is not unlike the *hennin* that was very popular with ladies in the fifteenth century. In Calais the head-dress is pleated and starched, and forms a halo around the face. A similar one is found in Champagne, but this is smaller and made with two layers of gathered lace and threaded with ribbon, the two ends standing up in front. In Alsace, the head-dress consists of a large silk bow in red or black.

The men's costumes do not show such a wide variety of styles as those of the women. Very popular are the loose-fitting worker's smocks, often in blue and sometimes white or checked as in Bresse. Trousers are usually dark but can be checked or striped. Knee-breeches are also worn and are found in Savoy, Nice, Poitou and Lorraine. In Lyonnais, leather gaiters button up to the knee; in the Île-de-France, bright striped stockings add a touch of colour.

There are many variations on waistcoats, jackets and shirts. In Alsace the waistcoat is red or pink brocade and is worn under a short black jacket with two rows of gold buttons. In Normandy the men favour a brocaded waistcoat in yellow or gold. There is also a wide variety of hats. Peaked caps are very popular, as are berets, while top hats feature in Savoy and Périgord. There are straw hats, especially in the

*Wooden sabot from Vallée de Bethmale, Pyrenees.*

summer, flat-brimmed felt hats in many regions and also the pull-on stocking hat.

Wooden sabots were once worn in most areas, being replaced on Sunday and festival days by a black outdoor shoe. In the south, canvas-topped espadrilles or a lightweight slipper replace the heavier sabot of the north and central regions.

The region of Brittany is very different from the rest of France as it is Celtic in origin. The Bretons speak their own language, and are very protective towards their ancient Celtic culture. The music, dances and costumes of this region are very distinctive and unlike other parts of France. There are many interesting and unique festivals, some of them connected with the sea. In some of the villages on Sundays costumes are still worn for going to church, as well as for special occasions such as weddings and festivals.

A costume from Finistère is interesting: the black bodice has a simple round neckline and long wide sleeves, all of which are covered with a fine silk braid in gold or in deep orange. The patterns executed on the bodice and sleeves are extremely old and the circular designs reflect their Celtic origin. The skirt is black and a large

*Breton lace coif.*

FRANCE. *This couple is from Provence in the south of France. The little girl is from Arles and is wearing a costume known as the Mireille, which evolved in the middle of the nineteenth century. Women wear the same costume but their skirts fall to the ground. The skirt can be in a variety of colours: pale blue, shades of green, white or dark red, and is made either in silk or a patterned brocade. The white cap of ribbon or lace is known as a cravate and is worn with a special hair style. The hair is parted down the middle and the two side-pieces drawn back and combined with the back hair, forming a bun on top of the head. A comb holds the hair in place and the long, white triangular cotton cravate is tied around the bun, the ends forming a little bow in front. The man's costume is very simple: white trousers and shirt, a wide coloured sash with the ends tucked in and a dark, patterned, sleeveless waistcoat. He comes from Basse-Provence and the waistcoat would be either floral-patterned velvet or silk brocade. The trousers are usually white but can be pale beige or brown. A red, blue or black sash is tied around the waist. The black hat has a dent in the crown and is known as a Frivole. Black leather, lightweight shoes, sandals or rope-soled espadrilles are worn.*

white brocade or embroidered satin apron is worn over it. The coif is like a chimney-pot made of stiffened lace. Black leather shoes have now replaced sabots.

For many years the men in Brittany wore full, baggy, white linen trousers called *bragou-braz*. These full trousers were fitted into long gaiters and were not unlike those worn in the Netherlands and Sardinia. However, they have now been replaced by the more fashionable long trouser in dark blue, black or finely striped black and white.

Many of the men's costumes are based on a sleeved jacket over which is worn a sleeveless waistcoat in the same colour and design as the jacket. Sometimes the waistcoat and jacket are contrasting. In Pontivy, the jacket and waistcoat can be in a black and white design while, in Elliant, gold embroidery in a Celtic design of leaves and flowers is used. Embroidery on the jackets and also on the waistcoats is a feature of most of the men's costumes.

Provence is often described as 'the king-dom of the sun', and the climate has given a special quality and elegance to the costumes of the women, reflected in the colours and materials used. In Haute Provence the gathered skirts are of flow-ered cotton in pastel shades. The long-sleeved bodice can be either black or white and a fichu or shawl is draped across the shoulders and fastened at the waist-band in the front. The apron is gathered into a small pointed basque and can be either black or white. In Basse Provence the skirt is sometimes in two stripes which have a combination of blue/red or yellow/white. A full-sleeved blouse is worn and the apron and fichu are white. Attractive little white bonnets, which vary according to the area, are worn: they can be tied under the chin, crossed under the chin and tied at the top of the head or the ends just left loose.

# BASQUE

THE BASQUE REGION is partly in France and partly in Spain. It is situated either side of the rugged Pyrenees, where these mountains slope down to the Bay of Biscay. The origin of the Basques is unknown, and their language appears to have no affinity with any other European tongue. In fact, it is claimed that they are the oldest race in Europe. They are proud, strong and hard-working people with characteristics unlike either the Spanish or the French.

The basic costume of the Basques is simple, apart from one or two exceptions. The men in the French section wear white trousers and shirt, a red sash and beret, with rope-soled canvas shoes tied around the ankle with red lacing. In France the shoes are called espadrilles, but they are not always worn and canvas shoes may replace them. For several dances such as the sword dance, sticks, and other ritual dances the men wear a pad of bells around their calves, rather like the 'ruggles' worn by English Morris men. A red waistcoat worn with a green sash is also popular. For the famous *mascarades*, in Soule, five men wear very colourful costumes as they dance over and around a wine glass. In *La Danse des Volants* the men have long, red, yellow and green ribbons fixed onto their backs and wear a head-dress that is similar to a bishop's mitre.

The woman's dress is as illustrated. Popular for dance presentation is the costume that is based on those worn by fisher-women. This consists of a blue dress with short sleeves, a black apron and a white, cotton shawl draped across the shoulders and tucked into the waistband. A white handkerchief is worn on the head and tied at the back. The material can be plain blue, or navy blue with little white spots.

The men and women in the Spanish Basque Provinces wear very similar costumes to those of their French neighbours. The women have full red skirts, but often without the black bands around the hem. The apron is black, as is the bodice. Sometimes a black skirt is worn over the red one and this is tucked up on one side to show the red underskirt. The white handkerchief is tied at the back of the head in the same manner as the women in the French area. The apron may have a little pocket and a small white handkerchief is placed into it. The man's costume is as illustrated.

One man is dressed as a hobby-horse. Another character, the Man-woman, is dressed in a red skirt, white apron, blue jacket and a hat. The man called the Cat carries a wooden trellis that opens and shuts while the Sweeper has a stick with a horse's tail on the end of it. The Cat wears a blue jacket and knee-length yellow trousers, white stockings and spats and the Sweeper is in red with similar trousers, which are black. The final character is the Flag-bearer in a black suit.

*BASQUE. This couple are Basque dancers, the man from the Spanish region and the woman from the French region. The woman wears a full red skirt with a white petticoat underneath. The skirt is usually worn without an apron although the Spanish women prefer to wear a small black one. On her head she wears a white scarf, which is tied at the back of the head with a bow. Her stockings are white and worn with rope-soled, canvas espadrilles. These can be tied around the ankles with red laces or criss-crossed up the leg. The man wears knee-length, black velvet trousers underneath which he wears a type of Spanish pollollos or white under-trousers. His thick, hand-knitted, patterned stockings have a garter under the knee. Alpargatas, the Spanish rope-soled shoes, have been replaced by a leather version with lacing crossed over the foot and tied around the ankle. In the Spanish region a black beret is worn but in France it is always red.*

# BELGIUM

THE COSTUMES WORN IN BELGIUM are often very simple, both in style and design, and owe a lot to French, German and Dutch influence. The colours tend to be darker in the Flemish regions and brighter in the Walloon area.

The costumes worn by Flemish women have full, striped skirts with an added frill at the hem. The colours are usually dark blue or brown. The bodice is plain in colour, made either of cloth or silk, and fastens up to the neck; sleeves are long. Another touch of colour is added by the wearing of a Paisley shawl. These shawls became very popular in the nineteenth century when Scottish weavers developed those patterns depicted on material from Kashmir; the curved designs are based on the Indian mango shape. The bonnet is made of the white lace for which this region is famous; it either has earflaps or two long streamers that hang down the back.

The Walloon girls also wear full skirts, with stripes ranging from a rather sober combination of greys, black and browns, to much brighter colours, but no frills are added. The bodice is cut as in the Flemish costume, but is of a brighter colour; the Paisley shawl is also worn. The Walloon girls wear an apron which can be either large with horizontal stripes, or small and of a plain colour. At Stavelot a poke bonnet of yellow straw is worn, called a *chapeau à bavolet*. It is decorated with check ribbons and a white frill across the back, which protects the neck.

The men in both regions wear a blue linen smock, similar to that found in neighbouring countries. In Flanders it is very full and in the Walloon it is pleated,

BELGIUM. *This couple are wearing costumes from Flanders, the Flemish-speaking region in the north. The women's skirts are inclined to be rather dark in colour in this area. The shawl can be worn crossed over in front and tucked into the* *waist, or the ends may be left hanging. The man wears a blue smock, which is gathered and full; in Walloon it would be pleated. Smocks in both areas would be made of linen. A black or dark blue peaked cap is common to both regions*

with a yoke. A shirt, fastened at the neck with coloured ribbons, is worn underneath, or the smock can be buttoned right up and then a red spotted handkerchief is worn. Dark trousers and a black or dark-blue peaked cap complete the costume.

Sabots have now been replaced by shoes; sometimes the girls wear leather bootees.

The costumes illustrated are now only worn by folk groups, although in some of the country areas the smock can still be seen.

# GERMANY

WITH THE ABOLITION of the German Democratic Republic, East and West Germany became united into one country. The country we now know as Germany was at one time a patchwork of kingdoms, electoral principalities, grand duchies and duchies. It was only natural that strong individual traits should have given rise to the great range of costumes found in Germany today. Many of the costumes reflect the styles of neighbouring countries: Denmark to the north, the Czech Republic (formerly Czechoslovakia) to the east, Austria to the south-east and France to the west.

The Baltic and Scandinavian areas also influenced the northern costumes of Germany. The material here is mainly wool, which helps to give protection to those areas exposed to the Baltic climate. Women favour red, blue, green and yellow for their costumes, which are popular Scandinavian colours. However, sombre colours are also used such as black, blues, greens and purples. The red skirts may be pleated, having a band of blue above the hem. The skirts are worn with a dark-blue, long-sleeved jacket. Alternatively, a red and green skirt with a dark-green jacket may be worn. The blouse worn underneath has a white frilled collar that shows above the neckline. A short cape fastened around the shoulders gives added protection against the weather. Plain-coloured or perpendicular-striped aprons are worn and red stockings are very popular; for weddings the stockings are red and yellow. Green ribbons tied in bows beneath the knees act as garters. A little blue bonnet with a bow at the back, similar to the Danish head-dress, is worn over a white under-cap. Older women wear a dark blue or black bonnet.

In the Mecklenburg lake district, a region halfway between the Baltic and Berlin, the women wear longer skirts and darker colours. A brown, long-sleeved jacket is worn with a black skirt and the cape is replaced by a green shawl which is crossed over and tied at the back. Away

*GERMANY. The woman on the left comes from Spreewald in the south-east. This is a picturesque forested region well known for its many costumes, traditional dialects and customs. A feature of this costume is the large padded head-dress called a Lapa. This is made from one large square silk or cotton scarf plus two smaller ones. The scarves are embroidered, edged with lace, and folded and pinned onto a stiffened base. The Lapa can be white or any pastel shade with a matching or contrasting shawl and apron. Skirts vary in colour and can be black velvet to match the bodice, or red with a band of black. The woman on the right wears a costume that comes from the old region of Brandenburg and shows a blend of styles from neighbouring countries. The blue apron has braces which fasten onto the waist-band at the back, and give a Bavarian feel to the costume. The pleated skirt and frilled blouse are similar to those worn in the Czech Republic. The dark-blue sleeveless bodice has a high, round neck, which is a style found in several costumes in other parts of Germany.*

from the Baltic winds the hats become more frivolous and a little straw hat is tied on with black ribbons with a black drape down the back.

Further south and west of Berlin, the styles change and are more influenced by city fashions. High-necked, sleeveless black velvet bodices are worn over white long-sleeved blouses with frilled collars. The frills vary in size and can be quite large. Sometimes the bodice is patterned with flowers. The skirts can be striped in red or green, or pleated in red with a black border. Large black aprons are worn and the stockings are white. Little red bonnets with ribbons falling down the back tie on over a white lace under-cap.

In the Harz mountains, full black skirts are covered by long white aprons embroidered in yellow and tied at the waist with a yellow ribbon. A long-sleeved black bodice is worn with or without a coloured shawl, which has the ends tucked into the waist. Several rows of gold necklaces brighten the black bodice. A little cap with long black ribbons down the back or tied into a bow, similar to that worn in Alsace, is worn. White stockings and black low-heeled shoes, the type of footwear found in most regions, are worn.

Men's costumes are based on the frock-coat that was popular in the nineteenth century. In the Baltic region they are blue with a red lining and have lapels and a collar. The buttons are silver and underneath the coat a blue waistcoat is worn. Breeches are of yellow buckskin or made of wool, and the black leather boots are knee length. A white collar is worn with a black silk bow. A broad-brimmed felt hat has ribbons at the back, but top hats, decorated with flowers and green ribbons, are worn at weddings.

In Mecklenburg the blue coat is cut without lapels and the breeches are replaced by yellow trousers worn with purple stockings and black shoes. A high-necked green woollen waistcoat is fastened with a double row of buttons. A black scarf is tied around the neck, while a black top hat is also worn.

In the Berlin area the costume consists of a red-lined, blue coat without lapels, yellow breeches, high boots and a blue waistcoat with a double row of buttons. A black scarf is again tied round the neck, and the black top hat has a buckle in front.

In the Harz region, a countryman would wear black breeches tucked into gaiters. The blue frock-coat is lined with red and has brass buttons or silver for Sundays; the high, patterned waistcoat is similar to that of other areas. Black shoes are worn.

The relaxed way of life of the southern Germans and Rhinelanders is shown in their costumes and the use of colours, as well as their dancing; brighter colours are used for skirts, bodices and aprons, with red and yellow strongly featured.

The Germans have a great love of music and a fondness for carnivals, festivals, folk dancing and other folklore occasions for wearing costumes. Peasants from the Ries Plain, the inhabitants of the Black Forest and of Bavaria still wear their native costumes when they come into the towns on market days or for the many festivals.

Women's costumes show numerous ways of wearing bodice, blouses, skirts and aprons. The bodice, known as a *Laibli* or *Leibli*, can be sleeveless and fastened down the front, the neck edge, armholes and front fastenings being decorated with braid, velvet or pleated ribbons; the bodice can be quite plain or embroidered with a pattern of flowers. In some areas sleeves, made of the same material, are attached to the bodice, while the cuffs, neckline and front fastening are bound with velvet of a deeper shade. A very attractive bodice in black velvet and edged with braid and

GERMANY. The little girl is from Hesse in central Germany and the woman who is with her wears a costume from the Black Forest. There are many attractive costumes in the Black Forest region, and they can vary from village to village. A feature of many of them is a decorative yoke called a halsmantel or halsband.

This was originally separate, fitted over the bodice and was kept in place by four ribbons attached at the corners and tied in bows under each arm. Now it is part of the costume. As in this costume, the halsmantel can be edged with embroidery or braid; they vary considerably according to the district and village. The skirts are often sombre, and are frequently black. In some villages the skirts may be pleated or striped, but they are usually in plain colours. The most interesting feature of this costume is the hat. The straw hat is worn over a little black cap, and the crown of the hat is decorated with woollen pompoms. Red denotes an unmarried woman while black denotes marital status. The little girl wears numerous petticoats which are worn over a padded roll tied around the waist. The first petticoat is a a narrow, or modesty, petticoat that prevents the legs being shown too much during some of the boisterous dances. The skirt is woollen and the apron is made of white cotton. The stockings are tied under the knees with red garter ribbons. A tiny head-dress, made of ribbons on a round stiffened base, is fixed on top of the hair.

pearl buttons comes from the Black Forest. A blue or green bodice edged with red braid is another colourful variation and is found in the south. In the region bordering Switzerland bodices are laced across with coloured ribbons, leaving a wide gap in which a panel of plain or embroidered velvet is worn, and underneath this is a blouse.

Aprons are worn in most regions, but tend to be plain in the north and flowered, braided or embroidered in the south. German costumes are not embroidered a great deal; embroidery is found on bodices, hems of aprons, and front panels and yokes, although not in great profusion.

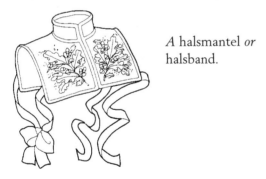

A halsmantel or halsband.

One of the important features of German costume is the hat, each region and village having a different style. In the area near Alsace, a large bow type of head-dress is worn, similar to those worn across the border. If a girl is unmarried, she wears a plait down her back, but married women tuck their hair into little black caps worn underneath the bow. There are also tall hats, little hats made from ribbons, hats with eye veils, hats decorated with ribbons on the crown, hats denoting religious denomination and the very lovely bridal

crowns or *Schappel*, made of flowers, ribbons, beads, pearls and glass.

The young girls wear their hair in plaits or plaited and bound around the head and, on special occasions, plaited with ribbons. Stockings are white and the shoes usually black.

Many of the men's costumes are similar in style to those found in other Teutonic countries: knee-breeches, waistcoats, jackets, shirts and hats with variations according to region. The knee-breeches are often black or of a dark colour, with embroidery on the front flaps and on the sides. The breeches in the north tend to be plainer and those in the south a little more decorative. In Bavaria the breeches are replaced by leather shorts common to both Germany and Austria.

Waistcoats are worn in most regions but vary considerably in design. They can be double-breasted, fastening up to the neck by means of two rows of gold buttons: sometimes the upper part is turned back to form lapels and revealing the shirt underneath, which is worn with a knotted scarf. A single-breasted V-neck waistcoat is sometimes worn and in some villages along the Rhine a type of sleeveless vest or pullover is very popular. This garment, scarlet in colour, has a round neck decorated with black velvet braid. Scarlet waistcoats, vests and shirts look very striking when worn with the black breeches, jackets or coats.

The wearing of scarlet denotes that the wearer is married: white is worn only by bachelors. In the south, gaily decorated braces are found and again marital status is denoted by the embroidery: if executed in white then the wearer is married, if in red then the wearer is still single. Also, a

GERMANY. This couple wear costumes typical of Bavaria, which has strong links with Austria in the designs and materials used. The woman wears a black bodice tied across the front with a silver cord or chain that passes around silver hooks. The fringed shawl is of wool or silk and the ends are tucked into the top of the bodice and fixed with a posy of flowers. Several white petticoats are worn under the red woollen dress, which has a full skirt to allow plenty of movement for all the turning dances. The black felt hat is trimmed with gold cord and either a flower, or perhaps an eagle's feather, is worn. There are variations on this costume – the skirt may be black and the apron may have a floral pattern. The man is wearing the very popular short leather lederhosen common to both Bavaria and Austria. When the waistcoat is not being worn the broad, decorated braces with a cross-band would be visible. The dark green or black hat is decorated with a chamois plume. The knitted stockings are white and end at the ankle – they have no feet. This type of stocking evolved as heavy shoes continually wore holes in the toes and heels of the socks. It is in this costume that the men dance the famous Schuhplattler.

married man turns the brim of his hat up and the unmarried has his brim down.

Long-sleeved jackets reaching to the waist or hips and decorated with one or two rows of buttons are worn over the many kinds of waistcoats. These jackets can be black, brown, red or blue and are often lined with a contrasting colour. The buttons can be of silver, shaped like a coin or, alternatively, carry a design. In the north the jackets reaching to below waist level are cut straight to the neck with a round edge or slight stand-up collar.

In the Schalm Valley and on the Ries Plain, a large blue smock is worn, which has white braid on the shoulders and around the neck. This garment has its counterpart in France and Switzerland and is very reminiscent of the basic European tunic. White shirts are worn in most areas with flat or stand-up collars, together with red or black bows or knotted ties.

Black top hats with a green head-band fastened in the front with a buckle are found in many areas. Black, round beaver hats with varying sizes of brims curling inwards are also popular and in the north a black tricorne is worn. At one time wood-men working in the forests used to wear black varnished straw hats with square crowns, their hat denoting their craft. White or black socks worn with silver buckled black shoes are the most usual footwear for men.

# AUSTRIA

WHEN AUSTRIA LOST HER EMPIRE in 1918 a strong nationalist feeling developed in the country with a revival of peasant costumes and dances. With the coming of the Salzburg Music Festival the dirndl dress was created. This is now the most popular costume. Basically it is a full skirt, with a bodice of either wool, cotton or velvet that is laced or buttoned up with silver buttons. A white short- or long-sleeved blouse is worn under the bodice. On weekdays plain or coloured cotton aprons cover the skirts, but on Sundays silk aprons are worn. The dirndl differs in colour, materials and design, and can be simple or elaborate. There are regional variations in the bodice neckline.

Men have a costume which is also very popular and is worn by young and old alike. There are two styles, the lederhosen – chamois leather shorts or breeches – and the long woollen suits. Lederhosen are probably the most practical form of trousers in existence, and are thought to have been originated by the Celts. Grey or black in colour, they are worn with embroidered braces and ornamental belts.

AUSTRIA. Both people are wearing typical costumes from the Tyrol. The woman is dressed in a dirndl-style costume; from the flask at her waist she pours some brandy for the man. The woman's full skirt would have several white petticoats underneath. This design is very simple but it is the basis of numerous Austrian costumes; variations on the style of the bodice and the colour of the apron and skirt can be found throughout the country. The man wears breeches made of leather or loden. The jacket may also be in loden, and made in different styles. The red waistcoat is decorated across the top. The men often replace the waistcoat with cross-bar braces. The belt is made of leather and elaborately decorated. The black felt hat shown here is very plain – frequently a feather would be in the hatband or the hat would be larger and decorated with long tail feathers.

The short style is usually worn for dancing or by young boys. A white open-necked shirt with rolled-up sleeves is worn, occasionally with a tie. White stockings and black shoes complete the costume.

For more formal wear coats, jackets and trousers are made from a thick woollen felt-like material called *loden*, in grey, green or brown. It is very warm and weatherproof.

Skirts in all of the regions are full and often pleated. In the Tyrol, skirts are usually red or black and gathered rather than pleated. In the state of Burgenland skirts are white with a slight pattern, similar to those worn in Hungary. The skirts worn in Carinthia, the most southern state, are all accordion pleated; black and brown are the most popular colours, the hems being edged with a green or coloured border. Embroidered belts with bunches of coloured ribbons hanging from the waist are worn.

Many of the Austrian dances are couple dances that involve a great number of turns, so several white cotton petticoats are worn under the skirts. In the Tyrol red and green bodices are worn over white blouses and in the east the bodices are dark and the blouses are long-sleeved. In Upper Austria at Innviertel a tight-fitting plum-coloured jacket with a basque replaces the bodice. The full skirt is in the same colour and a gold shawl is draped over the shoulders.

Some of the regional costumes have long-sleeved bodices and skirts made in the same material. Those from the Ziller Valley are in black with a square neckline and gathered sleeves. In the Lower Inn Valley the dress is in maroon and in Wachau, Lower Austria, it is made in gold or blue brocade with a draped neckline. Blue, green, gold and orange aprons are popular, and for Sunday wear they are often made in silk or brocade.

There are many different hats: in Salzburg little round felt boaters have a gold cord around the crown with two tassels. The women of Innviertel wear a strange gold hat that fans out like a bird's tail. In Wachau the hat opens out like a halo. In Vorarlberg the children wear a golden crown tied on with black ribbons and the women wear fur hats. When the French Army was retreating in 1809, many of Napoleon's men threw away their caps and these were retrieved by village girls, who wore them to mock the former victors and thus a new fashion was created.

White, blue, red and green stockings knitted in a rib or another pattern, are worn with silver buckled black shoes laced with red ribbons. In Burgenland the stockings and ankle boots are black. In this region the men wear breeches made of wool or leather, in black, brown or grey. These leather breeches will often have a design worked on the wide seams or the front opening. Red waistcoats are very popular and are fastened with either a single or double row of silver, brass or horn buttons. In the Tyrol the waistcoats are made with round necks and have side fastenings. Decorated broad leather belts and braces are worn over these waistcoats. In the mountain regions the colder weather demands thick breeches with waistcoats and jackets made from *loden* material.

Jackets vary in colour and can be blue, brown, green or grey. In Styria the grey jacket is short with a green collar, cuffs and lapels. In Upper Austria the jacket reaches to below the hips and is similarly decorated. In the Salzburg region the jacket is green and reaches to the hips. On most of the jackets the buttons are of silver or horn.

The Tyrol is an area that provides much of the wool, leather, horn and silver used in the making of costumes. At one time it was reputed that the miners were so rich that the nails in their boots were made of silver.

White shirts are worn with most costumes and have red or black knotted ties or bows. Hats are very popular and range from broad alpine felt hats to fur and the felt caps of Burgenland. In the Tyrol there is an arrangement of plumes from the feathers of the black mountain cock, the eagle and other wild birds. The bunches of feathers are fixed into the hat bands and are known as *scheibenbart*.

In the Salzburg region black or green hats have the traditional *gamsbart*, which is a chamois brush. Gold cord and two tassels decorate some black felt hats and complement those worn by the women. A posy of flowers is often fixed into the hatband. White, blue or green knitted stockings are worn with black shoes, either laced or with silver buckles.

# SWITZERLAND

SWISS COSTUMES show the influence of neighbouring countries as well as having a definite style of their own. In the seventeenth and eighteenth centuries Switzerland was renowned for her lovely silks, ribbons, braids and embroideries and these materials were incorporated by the peasants into their costumes. Designs and embroidery are very colourful, reflecting the wild flowers of the country.

The French influence is shown in the pastel shades used in dress and aprons. Striped or floral print bodices and skirts are worn with plain coloured aprons or a dark dress is worn with an apron of pastel stripes. Small lace fichus or fringed shawls are draped or tucked into the top of the bodice. Trim little caps or bonnets, attractive flat yellow straw hats or winged black lace hats made on wire frames are all very popular in the west. Black lace mittens extending to the elbows are worn when the bodice or blouse sleeves are short. The costumes are very neat and this quality is reflected in the dance steps and music of the western area.

The costumes from the German-speaking districts are less simple than the western style: colours are darker, for example browns, deeper shades of blue, black relieved by white, pink, green, blue or

SWITZERLAND. *The woman wears a costume from Emmental and Plateau in the canton of Berne. The bodice of black velvet is worn over a white blouse, which has very fine pleats in the front. The yoke, which was once separate, is now part of the costume but the silver clips and chains that held it in place still remain. The bodice is laced with a silver chain or white cord wound around silver hooks. The apron is of taffeta and the head-dress is made of horse-hair or net gathered onto a little cap. The herdsman is dressed in the traditional costume from the Appenzell and Toggenbourg regions. This area borders Austria and shows strong similarities in the design of its costumes. The yellow breeches are made of soft leather and across the left hip a handkerchief is tied. Handkerchiefs are decorated with patterns of the herd, the names of the animals or proverbs from the area. Silver chains with old coins at the end hang from the waist. The red woollen jacket is edged with braid and the square silver buttons are either plain or have a filigree design. Lapels are embroidered with a sun, a star or a flower. The leather braces have a cross-section decorated with a line of cows.*

striped aprons. The bodices are a feature of this region and bear a similarity to those worn in the Black Forest. A costume from Berne has a bodice with red back and sides, and a yellow centre-panel over which black ribbon is laced around silver buttons. The yoke, which stems from the German *halsmantel*, is edged with black velvet. In some of the costumes the *halsmantel* or collerette is still worn, while in others it has been incorporated into the bodice. In Germany the *halsmantel* is tied on with ribbons: in Switzerland, silver chains with filigree rosette attachments are clipped onto the front and back of the bodice. This decoration is found on many Swiss costumes.

Little flat straw hats, little black hats which sit on the back of the head, tied on with ribbons, and little hats like halos are very popular. Long- or short-sleeved blouses are usual.

The Italian love of colours is shown in the costumes in the southern region. A red bodice laced over a white panel and worn with a white blouse, a green skirt, a violet apron patterned with flowers on the border and a blue shawl edged with coloured bands tucked into the bodice is an example. Brightly coloured headscarves, knotted at the back, are preferred to hats.

On the Austrian border and in the Romansch-speaking region, skirts are accordion-pleated in red, blue, green, yellow and black. Bodices tend to be more elaborate: one from the Haute-Engadine in the Canton Grisons has a red, long-sleeved bodice with a black velvet panel, a little black cape and also a black apron, all embroidered with flowers using gold thread. A white frilled collar, amber beads

and a tiny skullcap complete this costume.

In Appenzell, tight-fitting black bodices are worn with brightly coloured skirts and, for festive occasions, a long-sleeved jacket with a spectacular collar of white pleated lace edged with black is added. It is here that the lovely head-dress made like two butterfly wings in black tulle, with a pleated white inset, is worn. White stockings worn with silver buckled black shoes are most common, but occasionally red or mauve stockings are worn.

The men in several of the cantons wear a hip-length, long-sleeved smock in black or blue, worn over long black trousers and a white shirt. The neck opening has a wide V-line with borders of floral embroidery repeated on the shoulders and cuffs. The white shirt is fastened at the neck with a knotted ribbon with pompoms at the ends. The working smock is plain white, fastened at the neck and with a hood for protection against the sun. This was the basic outdoor costume, but it is now out of fashion.

In Gruyère and the Oberland the herdsmen wear blue or black jackets with short sleeves: those from Gruyère are blue and have embroidered edelweiss on the lapels and a design down the edge. The men in this area carry a black embroidered shoulder bag holding salt for the cows to lick. Their white collared shirts have specially pleated sleeves in an horizontal design. The shirt is buttoned at the neck and no tie is worn. In Oberland the sleeves are plain and a little black bow tie is worn. Skullcaps of leather, felt or velvet, which are decorated with tassels, are worn but black felt hats are worn with the smocks. The shoes can either be laced or have silver buckles.

# ITALY

MANY EXISTING ITALIAN costumes, embroidery, designs, patterns of materials and dances stem from the Renaissance period. Before the unification of Italy under Victor Emmanuel, the various states had developed their own characteristics, customs and costumes and, consequently, there is today a great variation in the numerous costumes to be found.

In the north, the predominant colours are blue, green, purple and black; in the south, reds, greens and maroon colours are preferred and near to the sea there is a predilection for blue. Red is favoured by brides and married women. Heavy materials, such as damask, heavy taffeta and wool, are used for some of the skirts.

Blouses are made of linen or cotton, bodices and jackets of velvet and aprons of lace, silk, cotton, linen or velvet. Necklaces of coral, chains of silver or gold and filigree brooches are worn extensively.

In the north, many costumes bear a strong resemblance to those of the Tyrol. Skirts are full and covered by large aprons; plum-red or dark-blue aprons are worn over black or plum-red skirts. Bodices are very popular in Italy; in the north, they are sleeveless and made in red or green woollen material edged with a contrasting colour and laced up the front over a red panel. White blouses have full sleeves and a high frilled neckline with a black velvet cross-over ribbon pinned at the throat.

A costume worn by young girls at the Easter festival in Val d'Isarco in the Dolomites has a full black skirt covered by a large white lace apron tied in the front with a pink ribbon. The red bodice is edged with green and laced over a contrasting panel. The blouse with its little stand-up collar has a frilled yoke (similar to the German *halsband*). In the Val d'Aosta the bodice is replaced by a long-sleeved black or blue velvet jacket with an inset panel embroidered in gold.

Large-brimmed, black felt hats are decorated with a green hatband and a silver buckle and these are worn in several regions. In Val d'Aosta, a bonnet-type hat made of stiffened gold thread lace is worn. A similar hat is made in white lace, decorated with flowers and ribbons on the crown. Where a hat is not worn, the hair is sometimes dressed in a bun which is studded with silver pins. In Lombardy the pins are large and have filigree ends, giving a shimmering halo effect. Black leather shoes and white stockings are customary.

In central Italy in the regions of the Marches, Umbria, Latium, Abruzzi and Molise, there is great variety in costume. The skirts are long and made from home-spun material in black or, for special occasions, in red. Large aprons covering the skirts are made in blue, brown or white cotton or, alternatively, in a white floral brocade. The blouse is often made in the same material as the skirt and those from

*ITALY. This couple
are from Aviano, near
Venice, in the north of
Italy. The woman's
bodice is made of velvet or
a woollen material. The skirt
is in a black homespun wool. These
costumes are passed down from
mother to daughter and several deep,
horizontal tucks serve to shorten or
lengthen the skirt as needed. Several
petticoats are worn and the
stockings are hand-knitted in
cotton. From her waist the woman
may wear several coloured
ribbons, souvenirs of boyfriends.
At one time the women would wear
silver ornaments in their hair but, with changing
fashions, flowers are now mainly used. The man
wears black trousers; on the lower part of the
trousers are little green trimmings. The red velvet
waistcoat has gold buttons. If the couple are
engaged the man will wear a piece of ribbon on
his lapel which will be same as the one that he
has given his girlfriend. His green felt hat is
decorated with fresh flowers if it is in the
summer; otherwise the hat will have some
small woollen balls on the left side. Both hold
handkerchiefs, which are used in several of the
dances of this region.*

Scanno, Abruzzi, have a large full sleeve gathered into deep cuffs.

The most usual form of head-dress seen in central and southern areas is the *tovaglia*. Designed to protect the back of the neck and the head from the sun, it can be worn in many different ways. It is made from linen that is starched and folded to form a type of hat. In parts of the Marches it is folded into three, facing the back of the head, and is secured with pins. In Abruzzi, a lace or white scarf is first draped over the head and the material then folded across the top. In Latium, the edge of the white material is scalloped and embroidered in white, the flat upper front section being rolled under. The *tovaglia* is usually white, but if two are worn then the top one is heavily embroidered or coloured. The material, when folded, is kept in place by long pins with decorated ends. A silver pin is worn by young girls and a gold pin by a bride or married women. In Letino and Gallo Matese in the Campania, the women's head-dress is called the *mappelana*. If green in colour the wearer is unmarried and, if red, she is married: black denotes widowhood.

Towards the south skirts are pleated, black and red being the most popular colours. In Frosinore (Latium) two brightly coloured skirts are worn, the upper one being gathered round the hips and pinned under a dark apron, giving a pannier effect.

An unusual bodice with separate sleeves is worn both in Abruzzi and Molise; in black velvet

*An Italian* tovaglia.

and cut low in front, it is worn over a long-sleeved white blouse. A black velvet sleeve is then pulled over the blouse leaving a gap of 12.5–15cm (5–6in) between the top of the sleeve and the shoulder through which the blouse sleeve protrudes.

In Monteroduni (Molise) the sleeves and bodice are red velvet edged with silver braid; they are worn with a red pleated skirt and a black apron. In some of the regions of Molise the bodice sleeve reaches only to above the elbow. Blouses are made of white cotton and, when worn with a short bodice sleeve, the full sleeve of the blouse is finely pleated horizontally. Shawls or fichus of lace or floral material are tucked into the top of the bodice.

*Italian blouse sleeve.*

The shoe characteristic of the central regions is the soft black leather *ciocie*; one of the earliest forms of footwear, it is similar to a ballet pump. It has cross-lacing over the foot and is tied round the ankles and legs. White or black stockings are usual.

In the far south of Italy, in the regions of Puglie, Basilicata and Calabria, colours are more vivid and the skirts are fuller. Pleated

*An Italian* ciocie.

ITALY. This boy and girl from Naples are about to dance the famous tarantella. The girl wears several white petticoats under her blue silk or cotton skirt. The high-cut black velvet bodice is partly hidden by the wide collar of the blouse, and the bodice is tied with a large silk bow. The white ribbed stockings are worn with light, flexible shoes, necessary for the nimble footwork of this famous dance. The boy wears a gold brocade or velvet waistcoat over his white shirt. The red breeches fasten at the knees with silver or gold buttons. The fisherman's red hat is in a style found in most Mediterranean ports. Made of wool, it provides good protection in all weather as it clings firmly to the head. A broad sash is tied at the waist, the ends hanging down the left side. The waistcoat and breeches are always in contrasting colours.

skirts are still very popular, but the pleats are very tight and narrow at the waist and hips, opening into broader ones. The pleats are made by first dampening the material, pressing in the pleats and hanging the skirt up to dry. Under repeated processing, the pleats become practically permanent. In some areas of Calabria two pleated skirts are worn, both with a deep gold border. The upper skirt is folded back in the front and secured, or tucked under the arm.

In Taranto (Puglie) long-sleeved coloured jackets are worn with vividly coloured skirts. Jackets are tightly waisted and flounce over the hips. A triangular lace fichu partly covers the jacket front, reaching from the shoulder to a point at the waist. Dark-blue jackets partner red skirts, light blue with yellow, pink with blue, or green with brown skirts, thus giving many colour combinations. It is probable that at Taranto the famous dance, the tarantella, originated.

In Sorrento the dancers wear black or red velvet sleeveless bodices, cut low in the front and high at the back. White blouses have little puff sleeves and around the low and rather wide neckline is a large gathered frill. Skirts are made of a heavy red, green or black silk with a braided border or a design round the hem. The apron is of a very fine white lace, which allows the colour of the skirt to show through. White stockings are worn with black lightweight shoes with a small heel.

Men's costumes are simpler. In the north, Italy shares a border with Austria and the styles are very similar to those shown in the illustrations on page 52. They have black leather breeches or shorts, red or black waistcoats, broad black or green braces, wide belts and black or red jackets. The black felt hats are decorated with a bunch of flowers, small feathers plus two or four long white tail feathers from a mountain bird. The smaller Alpine hats have a red or black hatband with a tassel at the back.

Away from the mountain regions, the men wear long black trousers, waistcoats of velvet or wool in a variety of colours and designs. These are single-breasted with a row of gold or plain buttons. A silk or cotton sash is tied around the waist and in the north the ends of the sash are tucked into the trousers. A white linen long-sleeved shirt, sometimes without a collar, is worn open at the neck.

Towards the central and southern areas the men's costume maintains a similar style. Black, dark-green or brown breeches replace the long trousers and they are made of wool or velveteen. In some areas the breeches reach to just below the knees and are tight-fitting, fastened at the knees with two or three buttons or a coloured garter tied in a bow. In Taranto, light brown breeches reach down to mid-calf and are loose in style. Waistcoats trimmed with gold buttons are made of silk, velvet or wool: they are frequently the same colour as the trousers.

# ENGLAND

ALTHOUGH ENGLAND is a country rich in folklore, dance and traditions there is little variety in her folk costumes. Folk dancing, however, has always played an important part in the life of the people and English country dancing has influenced the dancing in many other countries. The dances of Canada and the USA developed from those brought over by the early English settlers.

The most well-known costumes are those worn by the Morris dancers. There are many speculations on the derivation of the name Morris. One theory is that the name comes from the Moors who invaded Spain in the eighth century, and that the dance was brought to England by soldiers in the fourteenth century, but this form of dancing was practised long before the Moors came to Spain and the pagan rituals were known in numerous countries.

Morris dances were performed only by men at certain times of the year, in teams of six or eight with a Squire and Bagman in charge. These dances had ritualistic and magical meanings associated with the awakening of the earth. The dancers carried either sticks, swords or white handkerchiefs. The theme of animal worship is shown in one of the oldest of the Morris dances that comes from Abbotts Bromley in Staffordshire, where the dancers carry the antlers of deer. The Morris men of Abingdon carry the head of a bull as their emblem.

An unusual costume is worn by the famous Britannica Coconut Dancers from Bacup, Lancashire. Here the tradition is for the dancers to black their faces, the anonymity of the dancers being all-important to the folk dance. They wear a black jersey, black breeches, stockings and clogs. A short white skirt or kilt, which has red bands on it, is worn over the breeches. A white sash is also worn over the right shoulder on the 'men's' side, or over the left on the 'women's' side. The 'men's' side wears red braid on the turban-like headdresses, while the 'women's' side wears blue braid. Women now take part in Morris dancing, and special costumes have been created for the various teams and dances.

The dress for English country dancing is fairly recent, though for many years peasant costumes dating from the eighteenth and nineteenth centuries were used for folk-dance presentations. The girls wore laced-up bodices, blouses, skirts with a pannier effect, and bonnets or mob caps.

The men wore the old country smock, very similar in style to those found in France, Germany and other countries. A unique feature was the embroidery on the yoke, shoulders and wrists, known as smocking. From the colour of the smock it was possible to tell the region of the wearer and, from the embroidery on the collar or side panels, his occupation or trade. At the yearly hiring at fairs the farmers could read the symbols on the smocks of those waiting to be hired.

# ENGLAND

ENGLAND AND IRELAND. *The man on the left is dressed in a typical Morris costume. Morris costumes change from team to team, according to the region and the different dance traditions. It basically consists of white trousers, a shirt and a pad of bells around the calf of the leg. The ribbons across the chest have a rosette or baldrick with the emblem of the team. The decorated hat may be of felt or straw. Red poppies are a sign of health, wheat is a sign of plenty and the blue cornflowers signify being unmarried. The white handkerchiefs waved by the dancers symbolize the gathering and scattering of magic and energy over the ground and crops. The Irish couple are wearing costumes used for dancing, which incorporate certain features of rural dress. The traditional cloak has now become very short and is only worn for decoration. Each school or team of dancers has its own variation and colour. Green is the most popular colour for both kilts and dresses as it reflects the green of Ireland as well as St Patrick's emblem, the shamrock. Celtic embroidery covers the front and the skirt. Both the cloak and the man's plaid are fastened on the shoulder by a Tara brooch. According to the dance, the shoes may be either soft or a specially made hard shoe.*

# IRELAND

THROUGHOUT ITS TROUBLED HISTORY a strong folklore has grown up in Ireland, together with a wealth of folk traditions. The people were very poor, but had a great sense of enjoyment so that weddings and funerals were occasions for entertainments that would last for several days. They believed in sending the dead soul on its journey with merriment and there was plenty of dancing, accompanied by a piper or a fiddler, together with much singing.

Life for the Irish peasant was not easy and clothes were simple and functional. Many went bare-footed or wore primitive shoes made from animal skins and these were still being worn at the beginning of this century.

The climate is damp and both men and women wore woollen cloaks, known as brats. These garments had an attached hood to be pulled over the head on a cold day and the cloak would be fastened to the shoulder or chest by means of a Tara brooch, or tied under the chin with a black bow of corded ribbon. These cloaks were worn all over Ireland in the seventeenth century, by rich and poor alike, and may still be seen occasionally in parts of Cork. The wool was particularly thick and durable, being resistant to the weather. Black, red, blue and grey were the most popular colours, particularly red as the madder root, found in many parts of the country, was used as a dye. A mother would present her daughter with a new cloak on her wedding day and this would be kept for special occasions, the old one being worn for going to market.

The Irish were at one time expert metal workers and used intricate Celtic designs, which are often reflected in their dances. Irish dancing is extremely popular and, as with Scottish dancing, is performed all over the world. The costumes that would be worn at a Feis were evolved fairly recently and were designed for the quick, neat footwork and leg action found in the choreography of Irish dancing. They are very elaborate and heavily embroidered.

# SCOTLAND

ALTHOUGH CLOSELY LINKED geographically, Scotland and England have their own highly developed characteristics. The Gaelic-speaking clansmen bore the surnames of their respective chiefs and later wore their colours or tartans.

The Scots, as in many other countries, had a tunic or shirt made from a coarse material and dyed the popular saffron colour, which had the added quality of being an insect repellent. In the extreme winter weather of the Highlands, a length of woollen material was wrapped around the body and worn by both men and women. This developed into the kilt and plaid and served two purposes, a warm outer garment by day and a blanket by night. The material was worn pleated around the lower part of the body and held by a belt and the remainder was draped over the shoulder, being pulled around the upper body according to need. By the mid-eighteenth century the lower half had become a separate garment known as the *feile beg* or little kilt.

During the Stuart rising of 1745, in support of Prince Charles's claim to the throne, the English forbade the wearing of the kilt, together with the playing of bagpipes and other traditional Highland customs, condemning these as being too nationalistic. The result was that 'trews' were worn, these being a combination of stockings and breeches, cut in cloth and mostly favoured by the upper classes.

It is uncertain when tartans were first used, but there is mention of them in the sixteenth and seventeenth centuries. In the eighteenth century they became recognized and acknowledged as identification between the clans.

The kilt is still worn by both Highland regiments and as part of everyday dress. There are two distinct styles of Scottish dress: the everyday and social, and the dress for evening wear, weddings and festive occasions. During the day the man wears a tweed jacket, usually lovat green, with his kilt, a white shirt, stockings to match the jacket and thick brown brogue shoes. The sporran is made of leather and is used as a purse and, in the past, also acted as a protection to the body. Women have no definite costume.

For evening wear or festive occasions, the man wears the costume as illustrated. Black evening shoes or pumps would be worn with this costume. To match the man's finery at a Highland Ball, the woman would pin her tartan plaid to her evening dress. If the wife of a chieftain or colonel it is worn from the left shoulder, otherwise from the right side. For Scottish country dancing, the man wears either the day or evening dress and the woman a short or long full-skirted dress and draped plaid.

SCOTLAND AND WALES. *The Scottish couple on the left are dressed for Highland dancing. The man is wearing a jacket called a 'Montrose', which can be black, green, blue or another suitable colour. Alternatively, the man can wear a jacket called a 'Prince Charlie'. His kilt is in a tartan, this one being the Buchanan, with stockings to match the kilt. A lace jabot is worn with a 'Montrose' jacket, but a bow tie with the 'Prince Charlie'. Footwear consists of black Highland dance pumps. The*

*woman's costume shows the very fine pleating of the kilt at the back. Her tartan is Stewart, and her jacket may be in black or a coloured velvet. The woman's Welsh costume on the right is made of wool, locally woven and dyed. The design of the costume is not old – it was evolved in the nineteenth century and based on those popular in the seventeenth and eighteenth centuries. The brown over-dress has a skirt that opens down the front, the edges of which are folded back to show the bright red underskirt. The red dye used to be obtained from cockles and the brown dye from certain rock lichens. The tall black beaver hat is worn over a white frilled bonnet.*

# WALES

ALTHOUGH WALES is physically joined to England, the Welsh, like the Scots, have developed their own characteristics. The Welsh language is particularly musical and the country is renowned for its singing and choirs. Each year an Eisteddfod is held, at which dancers, singers, poets and musicians compete. The breeding of sheep is an important industry in Wales and consequently wool is used extensively for clothing.

The illustration shows a woman's costume. The men wear breeches, usually of a dark colour, a waistcoat and a white shirt. Buckled shoes are worn by both men and women.

# CORSICA

WITH THE LIMITED natural resources available, the costumes of Corsica have remained simple as well as being durable and practical and are unspoiled by modern or outside influences.

On the coast an Italian influence is evident, but in the more remote of the mountain villages sombre colours are worn. Women wear longish skirts and dark, long-sleeved blouses or tight-fitting jackets. A black handkerchief or *mezzaro* is draped on the head, while everyone wears black leather shoes to resist the harsh mountain weather.

The shepherds and the men from the mountains wear black waistcoats and trousers made in hard-wearing corduroy or velveteen. There are many kinds of thick shirts, and broad red cummerbunds are also worn. Black berets or caps give protection to the head and strong black leather shoes protect the feet.

Several festivals are held in different parts of the island, and these occasions are good opportunities to see the local costumes.

CORSICA AND MALTA. The man on the left is from Corsica and is dressed in a costume for a local festival or a special occasion. The smock-type of shirt is gathered into a round, narrow yoke and is worn tucked into the trousers. A similar form of smock is found in many other countries although it is usually worn outside the trousers. The couple are from the island of Malta. The costumes are based on those popular in the nineteenth century and reflect the Italian and Sicilian love of colour. The woman's bodice, buttoned up the front, is worn over a very attractive white V-necked blouse, which is trimmed with Maltese lace. There is also lace on the apron.

The man can wear red, black, blue, white or striped trousers with a matching or contrasting waistcoat. The stocking cap is often worn by men connected with the sea. Both are wearing leather shoes, but these are often replaced by sandals.

# MALTA

FOLK COSTUME IS ONLY WORN now in Malta at carnival time or on other special occasions. The very old dress called a *faldetta* used to be worn by most of the townswomen, but it is rarely seen now; this costume, peculiar to Malta, is reminiscent of the large cloaks worn in North Africa and is known as 'the hood of shame'. It consists of a long length of black silk material that is gathered on to a half-circular wire frame. One end was held in the right hand so that the frame formed a hood over the head, while the left hand held the material which was draped around the body like a cloak. It is generally believed to have come from Sicily or Spain at the time of the Arab invasions, when it was customary for the women to cover their faces.

# SARDINIA

THE INFLUENCES OF SEVERAL civilizations are reflected in the speech, customs and costumes of Sardinia. The island is divided into four provinces and in each of these areas the costumes vary considerably.

There are numerous festivals, processions and equestrian displays, all of which are opportunities to display costumes, which are worn with great pride. Colours are very definite, such as red, white, black and brown with touches of blue, green and yellow, all of which express the unusual landscape of the island. Silver and gold is used in the making of bracelets, necklaces, chains, rings and filigree buttons. The latter vary in shape from town to town: in some villages they are made like the wild anisette or aniseed flower. The material used for clothing is the wool shorn from the island's sheep which is spun, dyed from recipes using local herbs and then woven by hand.

Floral designs only are used on costumes and the embroidery is executed in gold, silver and silk thread. A feature of the women's costumes are the beautiful skirts which are long, full and pleated. Many of the skirts are made in a button-through style with an opening on the right

SARDINIA. *The woman comes from Gavoi; her hand-pleated skirt is made with the pleats narrower at the waist and increasing in width towards the hem. The old method of pleating, known as* fatta a tabellas, *is still used. The pleats are loosely tacked in place and then the skirt is dipped into water and pressed under large stones. On her head she wears a red* copricappa, *which protects her from the sun or from wet weather. In some areas a black* copricappa *denoted that the wearer was a widow. The man wears an old-style costume from Nuorese that is very characteristic of Sardinia. Over his trousers is a short, gathered, black skirt made from the local, hard-wearing wool called* orbace. *This gathered skirt is not unlike the Greek* foustanella *and may reflect the influence of the Greeks when they came to the island. The traditional hat is a* birritta, *a long stocking type of hat made of wool or felt.*

reaching from the waist to the hem; they are fastened with gold buttons.

Red is a popular colour for skirts and many have a deep band of embroidery at the hem. Sometimes this band is hand-painted with a floral design. The pleated skirt worn in Sennori is black and has a deep band of white, embroidered with flowers emphasized by a deep-red band. The side opening is outlined with pale-blue ribbon. In Orgosolo the skirt is brown with a band of green and red at the hem, and from the mountain village of Bitti the skirt has alternate bands of floral designs.

White sleeveless bodices cut high at the back and very low at the front are worn in several costumes; the very full sleeves are gathered into cuffs ending in deep frills. In Seneghe the large sleeves are pleated, either horizontally or vertically, and are freshly pressed for each wearing. The costume from this village is very plain and devoid of embroidery, its main feature being the sleeves and the heavy gold neck-laces set with pendants and precious stones, which cover the front of the blouse. Gold bracelets and rings on each finger are also worn. In one village each gold ring is fastened to a gold belt by a long chain.

In Villanova the blouse is red, and high-necked with long tight sleeves. Twelve bands of gold braid circle the arm from the elbow to the cuff, each ending with a gold button on the outside edge. Over this blouse is a bodice of very fine red and black stripes, edged with black. The red pleated skirt has a deep border of embroi-dery at the hem.

Very unusual jackets are to be found in Sardinia: the sleeve is made with only an outer section, which fastens at the wrist over the full-sleeved blouse. This upper sleeve is decorated in many ways, ranging from gold braid bands to thickly encrusted gold thread embroidery. In Sennori the sleeve is also edged with a white lace frill and the blouse edged with pale blue.

Aprons vary considerably in size, colour and design, according to the village. They can be quite plain in black or brown or have a border of embroidery, either at the hem or around three sides. The apron can be of brocade and pleated or have wide bands of brocade on three sides and a red pleated centre-panel, such as found near Cagliari. Lace aprons are also worn and a pale-blue silk apron from Sennori is embroidered all over with flowers found on the island.

Head-dresses range from a simple white lace- or linen-draped mantilla to a type of red cape, edged in blue or a band of gold embroidery. Head-dresses made of folded or draped white linen all have a piece of material that passes under the chin; at one time this would have covered the mouth in the belief that it was a protection from malaria.

In Osilo, a *copricappa* or cape of red velvet with a deep white band of floral embroidery is worn. The thickness of the cape gives protection against the rain and the cold in this mountain village. A widow would wear a plain black cape and black pleated skirt, but with a red jacket.

The women of Ploaghe wear a blue and black brocaded cape with a large orange cross on the back dating from the fifteenth century, when a great plague swept through the island; the cross was invoked as a protection.

At one time Sardinian women wore

white hand-knitted stockings with beautifully embroidered shoes that matched their dresses. Now, red, black or white low-heeled shoes are worn.

Men's costumes have not changed much since early times. The full white linen trousers, called *burzighinos* or *crazzas* are gathered into a pair of black gaiters or leggings. The trousers can also be worn like a divided skirt reaching to mid-calf and without being gathered at the knees. Over the trousers is a short, gathered, black skirt. Waistcoats vary and can be single-breasted and made in brocade which has a dark background with a floral pattern or of black orbace. Gold buttons, either in one or two rows, fasten the waistcoats. In Samugheo, in the province of Cagliari, black velvet waistcoats have a square neckline with a design painted on the front and the edges are bound in red.

Several waistcoats are made with sleeves and are really more like a jacket. The sleeve is split along the inner seam from the shoulder to the wrist, where it is buttoned. In Desulo this type of jacket is made in red orbace. In Oliena the jacket is red but the sleeves are made in a similar pattern to those worn by the women: this sleeve consists of only an upper section, which has a floral design on a white background, and the jacket is reversible and worn according to the occasion.

Long-sleeved black jackets are worn over dark waistcoats, but they do not have split sleeves. A thick, sleeveless fur coat made from goat or sheepskin and called a *mastrucca* is made in various lengths and dyed black, brown or kept in its natural shade. In summer the fur is worn outside and in winter the fur is reversed.

White linen shirts have full sleeves and are fastened at the neck and cuffs with filigree buttons. In some villages the collar is worn down and in others it stands up and no ties or scarves are worn.

# SICILY

NUMEROUS FESTIVALS are held through-out Sicily and the costumes worn on these occasions reveal the Sicilian's love of colour. There are two types of costume, those that are truly Sicilian and those that derive from Albania.

The Sicilian costume is far less compli-cated than that with the Albanian back-ground. There is a strong similarity to the costumes found in the south of Italy and Naples region. Women wear full skirts of red, yellow, blue, pink or black, with several bands of coloured ribbons or braid around the lower half. In some areas small, semicircular or square aprons edged with braid or embroidery are worn: all are made in contrasting colours to the skirts. Bodices vary: there is a black velvet, strapless bodice laced or buttoned in the front that is worn rather like a corset. The bodice is cut high up to the bustline in front and fits well into the waist and onto the hips. This type of bodice is worn over a white blouse with a round low neck and full, three-quarter-length sleeves. The brightly coloured skirt has a short apron of a contrasting colour. In Palermo the black velvet bodice fastens up the front to the bustline and has straps over the shoulder. The white blouse has a round neck and short sleeves. Brightly coloured skirts are worn without aprons and a scarf is tied over the head and knotted at the back.

Bodices are replaced in some areas by tightly fitting sleeved jackets with gold embroidery on the front. A dark-red jacket and skirt can be worn with a white apron decorated with open-work embroidery; with these goes a high-necked white blouse. The jackets can be of contrasting colour to the skirts.

Hair is generally kept long, but head-scarves are occasionally worn. Coral earrings and necklaces, beads and bracelets are added decoration. The stockings are white and the shoes of light black leather.

The men wear black or dark-blue breeches fastened at the knee with silver buttons or red braid. Long-sleeved black jackets or coloured sleeveless waistcoats are worn over white, long-sleeved shirts which are fastened at the neck with a red bow. Red sashes are wound round the waist with the ends falling free. White stockings and lightweight black shoes are usual. The fishermen favour striped stock-ings with black, rolled-up trousers or loose breeches, a white shirt with a large, red, knotted scarf tied around the neck and a black or red stocking cap. Sometimes black leather boots or shoes are worn, but often they go barefooted.

SICILY. This couple are wearing the most striking and colourful costume to be found in Sicily. They come from Piana degli Albanesi, near Palermo. The inhabitants of this small town were Albanians who sought refuge from Turkish domination over five centuries ago. The woman's full skirt is made of heavy silk taffeta and has three broad bands of gold embroidery, done at considerable expense. Sometimes the skirt is embroidered with a gold floral design. The red sleeveless bodice is also decorated with gold embroidery. Red was thought to be a colour that eliminated bad influences. The man wears thick white trousers which narrow down to the ankles and have a black or braided stripe running down the seams. The red sleeveless waistcoat and sleeveless jacket are both covered with fine gold braid or embroidery.

# THE BALEARIC ISLANDS

## MAJORCA

The largest of the Balearic group of islands is Majorca. The name derives from the Romans, who called Majorca 'Balearis Major'. Minorca was named 'Balearis Minor'. Majorca is a beautiful island that possesses some spectacular scenery and is a very popular tourist centre. The costumes are simple, but individual and colourful.

Women wear full skirts of plain cotton and these can have floral patterns, stripes or, if the skirt is of a plain colour, then a striped or plain apron in a contrasting colour is worn.

As in many other countries the colours reflect the landscape. Yellow and white stripes are very popular and so are deep blue and green, reflecting the sea, sky and olive groves.

Men wear large, full baggy trousers gathered in at the knees. These can be striped or plain and are usually in shades of brown, dark orange, plum or blue. The waistcoats, in various colours, have brocaded fronts with plain backs.

## MINORCA

The basic costume of the Menorquins is very similar in style to those found on Majorca. The women wear full skirts with floral designs rather than stripes; the bodice is black, but the sleeves are long. The wimple style head-dress is made of the same material as the skirt, but is unusually long, covering shoulders, chest and the upper back. White petticoats, white stockings and black leather shoes with a small heel and a decorative buckle make up the rest of the costume.

The men wear tight black knee-breeches with a white, open-necked shirt, a coloured sash and a waistcoat either of a plain colour or in patterned brocade. The shoes are similar to those that are worn by the women. The island is renowned for its skill in shoemaking.

## IBIZA

The costumes worn in Ibiza bear no relation to those found in Minorca or Majorca. The women wear very full long skirts in black, dark blue or white, often with accordion pleating. A matching blouse is worn with round gold buttons hanging from the sides of the sleeves. A very large fringed shawl is worn rather like a cape, covering the front and the sleeves of the blouse and reaching to a point down the back. The shawls are of a heavy dark brocade or embossed velvet. A white or coloured scarf is tied under the chin and the hair is worn in a long plait at the back and tied with a large bow of coloured ribbons. Several long white petticoats are worn with white canvas *alpargatas* (rope-soled shoes) laced over black stockings.

THE BALEARIC ISLANDS. *The couple who are standing are from Majorca. The woman wears a full skirt in a plain colour but it could have been in a variety of colours and might be patterned or striped. Aprons are not always worn but when they are part of the costume they are knee length and in a contrasting colour. The head-dress is made of a fine cotton or lace and frames the face, falling softly over the shoulders and to a point down the back. The man's full, baggy trousers are gathered in at the knees, and his brocaded waistcoat has a plain back. The white stockings and black shoes are similar to those worn by the woman. The woman who is sitting is from the smaller island of Ibiza. The very full skirt is in fine accordion pleats. An important feature of the costume is the wearing of numerous gold chains and necklaces. These signify the wealth of the wearer and are cherished heirlooms. A white handkerchief is tied at the waist and on this is a pendant of a saint.*

*Man's waistcoat from Ibiza*

The men wear thick white cotton trousers, baggy at the waist and gradually tapering down towards the ankle. Around the waist is a black or red sash with the ends tucked in. A black or red waistcoat with lapels has a stand-up collar and across the front are three rows of filigree buttons loosely clipped to the material. The long-sleeved white shirt also has a stand-up collar around which is tied a red scarf. A red stocking cap with a black head-band is worn with the crown folded over one side. White canvas *alpargatas* are very popular and are worn with or without stockings. The castanets used in Ibiza are very unusual. They are large, cover the whole hand and are played with all the fingers.

# SPAIN

APART FROM THE COUNTRIES of the former Soviet Union, Spain has probably the greatest number of costumes to be found anywhere in Europe. The simplicity and austerity of some Spanish costumes compares vividly with the richness and brilliant colouring of others. Materials used range from velvets and brocades to satins, cotton and wool. The costumes of one province will bear no resemblance to those of its neighbours and even within a small area costumes can vary considerably. Although several of the provinces are discussed in this book there is such a wealth of costumes that only the most popular are described. The costumes of the Canary Islands are described on page 86, while those of the Basque region are discussed on page 41.

## *ANDALUSIA*

It was in this region that flamenco music and dancing developed and became synonymous with Spain. Three types of dress are used for flamenco dancing: a short flounced dress, a dress that has a long tail (the *bata de cola*) and a long dress with a frill or flounces at the hem.

The short dress has a tight-fitting bodice reaching to the hips and a full skirt of three or four layers of frills inside it. The dress can be of a spotted cotton material in a variety of colours, plain or floral patterned and with or without sleeves. The popularity of the dance has brought many variations and elaborate designs involving net, lace, taffeta and other fabrics. This costume is not worn by dancers alone but can be seen generally at the Easter Fair at Seville.

SPAIN. *These two dancers from Andalusia are dressed in flamenco costume. The long-tailed dress worn by the woman is a* bata de cola. *The frills of the dress are starched or lined to make them stiff, and manipulating the dress when dancing is a great art. The shoes have very strong heels, which are essential for the foot beats. The man wears tight-fitting trousers cut well above the waist with a* chaleco, *or waistcoat, and a short jacket. The white shirt has frills down the front; when dancing the man will often remove his jacket. The boots reach over his ankles and are made with elastic side-pieces to enable the dancer to pull them on and give support. A common practice is to have small nails with large heads hammered into the heels, to make a strong tapping sound.*

Another popular costume used for practice is the flamenco dress, or just the skirt. This fits the hips tightly and then flares out to ankle length. The skirt is often made in panels and has one or two frills around the hem. The top can be sleeveless or have three-quarter-length sleeves with a frill around the bottom. Alternatively, a blouse may be worn, knotted at the front.

The men wear a tight-fitting suit, which consists of trousers cut high above the waist together with a waistcoat and jacket. Black is the usual colour for the trousers. The waistcoat and jacket may match or be in a variety of colours. For dancing, the men will frequently prefer to wear only the trousers, waistcoat and a white frilled shirt. The high-cut trousers, worn with a brightly coloured shirt knotted at the chest, is very popular. The flat-crowned, straight-brimmed *Cordobés* hats are popular with all Andalusian men as they give good protection from the sun.

## VALENCIA

The women's costumes are made of silk floral brocade in pastel shades. An apron and fichu of fine lace embroidered with gold are worn. A large pink or blue bow keeps the fichu in place at the back, with another large bow to fasten the apron. The hair is dressed in a special style peculiar only to this province, with a large plaited bun at the back with two smaller buns in 'earphone' style at the sides. A large gold comb is fixed into the large bun with two smaller combs in each of the other buns. Large pins decorated with pearls and jewels are fixed into the hair and gold earrings are also worn.

White stockings and white shoes with small heels are worn.

Men wear tight knee-breeches with long-sleeved short jackets made in pale-blue satin. A red sash is worn with a white shirt and white stockings are worn with *alpargatas* which are laced and tied around the ankles. The hat is a pale-blue or white knitted skull cap, which has a series of tassels hanging down from the crown. There is also a long multi-coloured striped shawl or rug, which is draped over the shoulders. Occasionally men wear an older costume that has links with ancient Greece. This has short trousers made of white linen, pleated to resemble a divided skirt. A red sash is tied around the waist and an embroidered or brocaded sleeveless waistcoat is worn over a long-sleeved white shirt. A red or striped scarf, similar to a turban, is wrapped around the head. White or blue stockings are worn.

## CATALONIA

Women wear full skirts of a pastel shade with floral designs on them. The black satin bodice is edged with white lace and a white or black lace shawl is draped round the shoulders. Aprons vary and can be small and of black lace or larger in white with silk embroidery, or trimmed with lace. Black lace mittens and a large black hair-net or snood is worn on the head. White stockings and either a low-heeled black shoe or alpargatas are worn.

The men wear tight black knee-breeches with a black jacket and a white shirt with a red sash round the waist. The red cap is similar to the stocking cap or

SPAIN. *This couple is from Aragon in the north-east of Spain. Both wear costumes for dancing the jota. The full, gathered skirt has a floral pattern on a dark background but a brighter floral skirt may also be worn. The short apron is black and the cross-over fringed shawl is white. White ribbed or plain stockings are worn with rope-soled* alpargatas.

*The man wears a pair of short black trousers. Around his waist is a deep cummerbund which may be in red, purple or blue. Underneath his trousers he wears a pair of white cotton under-trousers or* polollos. *Tied around his head is a plain or plaid scarf, known as a* cachirulo. *The wooden castanets are worn on the middle fingers and played in a peasant style rather than the style of the professional dancers, who use their thumbs.*

Phrygian cap so popular around the Mediterranean. In Catalonia the men fold the crown under in the front. *Alpargatas* are laced around the ankle and up the legs over the white stockings.

## GALICIA

The women in Galicia wear full red skirts with one or two bands of black velvet around the hem, similar in style to those in other northern provinces. Over the skirt is either a small black apron decorated with black lace and jet beads, or a large apron completely covering the skirt. A type of cross-over shawl is worn tied at the back and this can be red or black, with a band of velvet and jet beads, though in some villages it is of white lace. The blouse is high-necked with long sleeves. A yellow or white handkerchief is tied around the head and knotted on the top. Materials used are heavy, unlike the cotton used in the south.

Men wear black trousers to below the knees and under these are white under-trousers, or *polollos*, which are tucked into the tops of high black gaiters. Silver buttons fasten the gaiters on the sides and there are also buttons on the outside trousers at the knees. A white open-necked shirt is worn with a waistcoat which is black in front, but has a plain-coloured back. A wide red sash is tied around the waist. There are black lace-up shoes and a triangular-shaped hat reaching to a point and a red pompom. The costumes of the men and women vary in colour and design from one district to another.

# PORTUGAL

THE MANY FESTIVALS of the Portuguese reveal a strong national spirit as well as their ability to express enjoyment and happiness. This exuberance is seen in their bright and colourful costumes and even the fisherman's garb is far from being sombre.

The women's skirts throughout Portugal are fairly full. Complicated head-dresses are not worn: scarves are draped loosely over the head with black felt hats on top; these have a flat crown and are used for carrying articles on the head. The hat is sometimes replaced by a pad, known as a mother-in-law. In the coastal areas shoes are rarely worn, except on special occasions when either shoes or backless mules are used.

A bride on her wedding day wears a black dress of velvet with an apron beautifully embroidered with gold and jet beads. On her head is a white lace mantilla and around her neck many gold chains and other ornaments.

In lower Minho and the regions below the Douro, the women wear full gathered skirts of red, pink or other coloured cotton and around the hips a broad red or black sash. This gives a curious line with a slight balloon effect between waist and hip. Over a white or coloured long-sleeved blouse a brightly coloured floral shawl is worn with the ends caught at the waist. A black felt hat with a brim is worn over a plain or coloured scarf. In Esposende a little mirror is fixed into the hatband: as the women waited on the shore for the fishing boats to arrive, the mirrors flashed in the sun and so helped the fishermen to guide their boats home.

The costumes from the fishing village of Nazare are known for the use of tartan. Each family has a different pattern and it is thought that tartan was brought by the Scottish soldiers who fought in the Peninsular War in the early nineteenth century. The Portuguese admired the tartan and wove their own patterns. The women in this area wear a gathered tartan skirt with either a plain or tartan apron, which may be short or fairly long. The simple short, or rolled-up, sleeved blouse can be white, floral or coloured. A floral or black scarf is draped over the head. The hat is a round black felt with a 'pork-pie' crown and a large black pompom on the side.

One of the most interesting of the men's costumes comes from Nazare, where the fishermen go barefooted and wear the tartan shirts and trousers so popular in this area. On their heads a black stocking cap is worn.

On the southern side of the Tagus are the lowlands of the Ribatejo, the centre of bull breeding. Here the men spend their lives in the saddle and are known as *campinos*. They wear distinctive costumes of black or brown knee-breeches, which have four gold buttons at the knee and three at the hip pocket. A sleeveless red

PORTUGAL. These costumes
come from Vianna do Castelo
in the Minho region of north
Portugal, and the woman's costume is
one of the most colourful found in Portugal.
The skirt is of homespun linen and wool woven
into stripes with red being the predominating
colour. It has a deep border of black with white
wool embroidery. The bodice, partly hidden by
the shawl, has an upper section in red and a
lower part in black, both parts being
embroidered with coloured
wools. The bodice laces up the
front and is worn over a white
linen, long-sleeved blouse with blue
embroidery at the neck, cuffs and on the upper
sleeves. Gold chains, pendants, coins, crosses and
hearts, together with other filigree ornaments, are
very popular in this region. The man's costume
consists of a black suit with a curved line of
white buttons on the jacket and sleeves. A red
sash is tied around the waist.

waistcoat is worn over a white long-sleeved shirt complete with a red sash with the ends tucked in. A special green and red stocking cap, the *verdegaio*, is worn only by the *campinos*. The stockings are white and the shoes black.

Two very unusual costumes are found in Portugal, one from Miranda do Douro in the province of Tras os Montes. Here the men wear a white, three-tiered skirt with frilled and embroidered edges. A brightly coloured scarf is tied around the waist with the ends hanging down. A black waistcoat is worn over a long-sleeved white shirt which is buttoned to the neck. Around the shoulders is draped a floral shawl with a fringed edge. A black felt hat is worn, decorated with flowers and ribbons. The stockings have a horizontal striped design and the ankle boots are black. This costume is only worn when a particular dance, similar to the English Morris, is executed.

The other unusual costume is only worn in July by the *sargaceiros*, or seaweed gatherers, at Apulia (Minho). A white woollen, long-sleeved coat or tunic reaching to below the thighs is fastened with a broad leather belt. Short trousers are worn under this and on the head a type of sou'wester, rather like a Roman helmet.

# MADEIRA

THE COSTUMES OF MADEIRA, known as the '*Pérola de Atlântico*' (the Pearl of the Atlantic), are simple but colourful. The Island is known for its many beautiful flowers and lush vegetation. These colours are reflected in the women's costume of red woollen skirt with bright stripes of yellow, black, white and green. Both men and women wear a type of boot called a *botacha*. These are made of white or tanned oxhide and goatskin, and are rolled down to above the ankle. The boots are said to be copied from those worn by the Baltic sailors who came to Madeira with the oak that was used for the wine casks. The soft boots also enabled the wearer to make a firm grip on the slippery mountain roads. White boots are worn without stockings.

The men wear a loose, white, cotton or linen long-sleeved shirt. Loose, wide trousers are white, calf length and gathered into a band or cuff that fastens with white buttons. A broad white or red sash is tied at the waist and a similar type of cap to those of the women is worn, except that it has two triangular pieces at the sides in the headgear.

PORTUGAL AND MADEIRA. *The woman on the left with the flowers is from Madeira and the couple are from the Algarve in the south of Portugal. The Algarve is a popular area for tourists, and the costumes here differ greatly from those of Minho. The full skirts are lighter, with two or three bands of coloured braid. The blouse is worn outside the skirt; when the short apron is tied around the waist it gives a fluted appearance to the hem of the blouse. A black felt hat is worn over a scarf and a flower is fixed into the hatband. The man's costume is very simple: black trousers, black sleeveless waistcoat, white shirt, black socks and black leather shoes. The felt hat is also black. The woman from Madeira wears a simple but colourful costume consisting of a full red wool skirt with yellow, black, white or green stripes woven into the material. A little red cape is draped around the shoulders or over the left shoulder. A type of blue skullcap, ending in a point, is worn on the head. Boots are made of beige, white or red soft leather.*

# THE CANARY ISLANDS

THE CANARIES ARE A GROUP OF islands in the Atlantic Ocean, near to the Tropic of Cancer. They consist of seven islands: Tenerife, Lanzarote, Grand Canary, Fuerteventura, Gomera, Hierro and La Palma. The perfect climate, beautiful scenery and luscious vegetation are another reason why they are also called the 'Fortunate Isles'. The costumes of each island vary in style and detail, but they are all very colourful and decorative.

On the island of Tenerife the women wear colourful striped skirts similar to those in Madeira. There is a great variety in colour as the material is woven individually at home. White petticoats are worn, and these have fine drawn-thread work at the hems – a feature found on several of the islands – instead of embroidery. Bodices are red and laced up the front; occasionally a black bodice is worn. Little, white short-sleeve blouses may have a small collar or an attractive frill threaded with red ribbon or may be just plain. The tiny straw hats are worn on top of a scarf, which is tied either at the back or under the chin; white or yellow are the usual colours.

The men wear black trousers that come to the knees, worn over a loose pair of white under-trousers. A side opening at the knee is laced up in red with red pompoms. The red waistcoat edged with yellow has a white back and the open-necked shirt is also white. A red sash is tied around the waist with long fringed edges falling on the left side. Black shoes are worn and white stockings now often replace gaiters.

The costumes on the island of Grand Canary are decidedly different from those of Tenerife. The women's costumes are

THE CANARY ISLANDS. *The little girl is from Tenerife and the couple are from Grand Canary. The little girl's skirt is drawn up on one side to show the white petticoat and the beautiful handmade drawn-thread work at the hem. The red laced-up bodice is worn over a white high-necked blouse with puff sleeves. A small white apron, white knitted stockings and black leather shoes complete the costume. The woman's costume from Grand Canary is very elaborate with a double skirt, the top one gathered up to the waist at the sides to give the* type of panier effect found in the costumes of the eighteenth century. The underskirt has a deep band of embroidery in a geometrical design. The edge of the top skirt, the tight-fitting jacket and the apron are all decorated with drawn-thread work. A small black felt hat is worn over a blue scarf which matches the skirt. The man wears white linen pleated trousers cut like a divided skirt, a costume similar to that seen in Valencia in Spain. White half-socks stop below the calf and small separate socks are worn with the tops turned over the shoes or ankle boots.

reminiscent of those worn in the late eighteenth century. The large skirts are gathered up each side to give a pannier effect. The jackets, with the scalloped edges, are always white, although the skirt and petticoat can be in a variety of colours. The skirt may be white, red, pale-blue or dark-green – colours that reflect the islands' scenery and vegetation. The under-skirt or petticoat is in a contrasting colour with the headscarf matching either the top skirt or underskirt. A typical dress would be a white jacket, a red looped-up skirt and a pale-blue underskirt together with a little white apron and a red scarf. The men wear a very old style of costume: white linen pleated trousers, cut like a divided skirt. This costume is found in many countries and reflects the type of skirt-trouser worn by the early Greeks and Romans.

# Czech Republic

In 1918, AT THE END of the First World War, Czechoslovakia was established, embracing Bohemia, Moravia and Slovakia. At the beginning of 1993 the country changed into the present two main administrative divisions: the Czech Republic and the Republic of Slovakia.

The costumes from Bohemia show many influences of the cultural contacts that this country had with Austria and the West. The women's skirts are full and often pleated, with an embroidered border at the hem. Colours can vary and the skirts may be plain and in a variety of colours: black, red, blue, white, pink, or sometimes in a floral pattern. In the north-east, the floral skirt was called the 'new world' and in South Bohemia 'George's vision'. Several petticoats are worn. A feature of the costumes are the lovely, large aprons that reach down to the hem of the skirt. Floral aprons, aprons in vertical stripes with a floral design or white aprons trimmed with lace all contrast with the plain-coloured skirts. Bodices are neat and cut rather low in front. They are worn over white blouses with elbow-length puff sleeves. High, round, frilled necklines are very popular. In some areas a floral-patterned shawl is draped over the bodice, completely covering it; the ends are tucked into the apron. A shawl and a cap were presented to a newly married woman at midnight on her wedding day. Ribbons are very popular and worn on the back of

hats, on the front and back of aprons and in the hair.

Men wear mainly yellow cloth or buckskin knee-length breeches with a variety of fitting waistcoats or loose jackets. Both are decorated with braid and silver buttons.

Moving eastwards into Moravia, the costumes become much more elaborate. There is a predominance of colourful and intricate embroidery, more decoration, elaborate head-dresses and numerous ribbons worn by both men and women. Women's skirts are fuller and made from floral-patterned materials, which are also used for the aprons. Skirts are also made in pastel shades of pink, yellow, blue or white, and are either gathered or finely pleated. The white, blue, black or yellow aprons are more elaborate and the bodices are decorated with embroidery. White blouses tend to have larger sleeves and the frill at the neck has a heavier emphasis. Embroidery using black or gold thread is used on the blouses and ribbons are used for decoration. Tight-fitting little bonnets are worn at the back of the head and also decorated with ribbons. Unmarried girls have the plait of hair down the back, married women tuck their hair out of sight. White or black stockings are worn with black boots or low-heeled shoes.

The men wear tight black, blue or red trousers with braiding on the sides, front and across the back. The white linen shirts have loose wide sleeves, embroidered or

CZECH REPUBLIC. *These lively young dancers are from Bohemia and show the typical features of costumes from this region. The woman wears a full skirt which may be either gathered or pleated. The pleats used to be made by wetting the material, pressing in the pleats, tying up the skirts and putting them out to dry or baking them in a cool oven. Very proud of their pleats and handiwork, the women would show off the skirts in the turning polka dances. Unmarried girls usually have their hair in a long plait down the back with a ribbon tied on the end, or the hair tied with a ribbon. The young man wears yellow cloth or buckskin knee-length breeches tucked into black leather boots. His waistcoat is decorated with braid and silver buttons. The front of his shirt, on a special occasion, has embroidery down the front in white stitching.*

decorated with drawn-thread work. The waistcoats vary and can be red, edged with gold braid and gold buttons, or of the small bolero type made either of brocade, embroidered, or black and decorated with large red pompoms. Two leather belts are worn across the waist and hips, and tucked into the belt or trouser pocket is a beautifully embroidered handkerchief which has

been made and presented by a girl friend. Boots are black and round black hats with rolled brims are decorated with bunches of flowers and white feathers. The feathers are difficult to find and there is great competition among the young men to obtain them. The wearing of this feather is a sign of manhood, but once married the feather is put away.

# REPUBLIC OF SLOVAKIA

IN 1993 SLOVAKIA became an independent country, which is now called the Republic of Slovakia. Costumes found throughout Slovakia are numerous and varied. There is a saying, 'You'll find a different costume beyond every hillock.'

Skirts are very full and often finely pleated. Several white petticoats are worn, the first being a tight modesty one to

prevent too much leg exposure during the fast-turning dances. The colours of the skirts can be bright, and range from white, black, yellow, pink and blue to finely printed floral designs. Many of the costumes have a strong Hungarian influence in the design, colours and use of embroidery. Slovakia shares a long border with Hungary, and 4 per cent of the population are Hungarian.

*SLOVAKIA. The woman comes from Slovakia and the man from South Moravia. Her very colourful costume has a full skirt with numerous petticoats underneath, which make the skirt stand out in a very wide circle away from her legs. The bodice is also in red and decorated with braid. This very elaborate costume has much in common with those found in Hungary, which borders Slovakia in the south. Ribbons are very popular as decoration in Bohemia,*

*Moravia and Slovakia. These can be worn, as shown, tied around the waist or, on some costumes, tied above the elbow and on the hat. The man wears a brown short waistcoat, decorated with studs and braid. His white embroidered shirt has loose open sleeves, a feature found in many Hungarian costumes. In the flap of his black trousers he wears a drawn-thread decorated handkerchief which has been made for him by his girlfriend.*

Aprons are large and reach down to the hem; some cover the whole skirt, which is only visible when the wearer turns round. There is a whole range of aprons, depending on the region. Some are black with a bright border that is coloured with braid in horizontal stripes while others are white and heavily embroidered. In western and central Slovakia many of the costumes have beautiful embroidery on bodices, blouses and aprons. Blouses have large sleeves with high necklines and frills.

In the south and central regions men wear white linen calf-length trousers, rather like a divided skirt, and strongly resembling the Hungarian *gatya*. The shirt is short, ending at chest level and showing a bare midriff. A broad leather belt is worn around the waist. This is a summer costume and the one they use for their vigorous axe dances.

In the north, the Carpathian chain of mountains separates Slovakia and Poland. The mountain costumes are very similar in both countries. The women wear a simple style of dress, devoid of elaboration, with plain or floral-patterned full skirts, fewer petticoats, plain bodices and white blouses. Soft slippers, called *kierpce*, are tied around the ankles. The men wear thick, white, long trousers with a black braided motif on the front. A deep leather belt, white shirt with full, loose sleeves and a black hat complete the costume. *Kierpce* are worn, and tied around the ankles over the trousers.

# POLAND

THROUGHOUT ITS TROUBLED history, Poland has kept its strong national identity and yet shows the cultures of both the East and the West. The costumes are very individual and each region has its own style. In the villages great pride used to be put into the making of the costumes, with each family weaving the material on its own looms. Wool, flax and hemp were chiefly used and textiles were hard-wearing. In some areas striped materials used in the making of women's skirts and men's trousers are traditional. There is a strong love of colour and the stripes are in red, yellow, green, orange, blue and mauve, all of which are used to good effect.

Women's skirts are full and gathered rather than pleated, many being in a striped or floral pattern. Several white petticoats are worn. High-necked bodices are embroidered with floral designs in silk or wool. In some areas gold and silver thread is used together with beads. Blouses are white, usually with long sleeves and varying necklines or small frilled collars.

POLAND. *The couple are from Lowicz in the centre of Poland, a region famous for its striped woollen material and colourful costumes. The women's bodice is of black velvet embroidered with beautiful beadwork. Over the full skirt is an apron in the same pattern. Tight, laced-up boots are worn, footwear which is very popular in Poland. The man's trousers are also striped in orange and green and are tucked into black* boots. *His black jacket is fastened with brass buttons, but often these could be black. The men's costumes from this area have a resemblance to the uniforms worn by the Swiss Papal Guard in Rome. Lowicz was for many centuries a separate dukedom governed by the archbishops of the ancient city of Gniezno. It is thought there is a strong link, introduced by the archbishops, in the design and pattern of the costumes.*

POLAND. *This couple are wearing very popular Polish costumes which come from Krakow. The woman wears a full floral skirt, which can be in a variety of colours but always with floral patterns. The white cotton apron is decorated with lace, but floral-patterned aprons are very popular or those made of fine white drawn-thread work. The man's costume has been* known in Poland for many centuries. In the eighteenth century it became accepted as the official military uniform. The red tassels on the sleeveless coat have their origins as military decorations from the Napoleonic Wars. The blue coat, or kontusz, is decorated with an embroidered design on the front panels. His distinctive hat is called a rogatywka.

From region to region details change considerably and a very characteristic feature showing variation in costume is the apron. Red or black laced-up boots are worn a great deal in Poland. In the mountain areas a soft leather moccasin type of shoe (*kierpce*) is laced up around the ankles.

Young girls have their hair uncovered and worn in two plaits tied at the end with ribbons. Floral wreaths are also worn, or headscarves. Married women have their hair tucked into caps. Strings of beads are worn which can be of coral, glass or wood and, in the Baltic region, of amber or 'sun stone'.

The men's costumes are as colourful as the women's, with striped or plain-coloured trousers tucked into red or black boots. Shirts are white with long sleeves ending in cuffs and these are worn with sleeveless waistcoats. There is a great variety of jackets, which are of various lengths, colours and styles. In the Krakow region the sleeveless coats are blue and reach to the knees. North of the region at Opoezno they are white and have sleeves. Further north in the Mazury province they are black.

Many of the men's costumes have a military cut and appearance, which may be the influence of the constant wars undergone by the country. The Poles are also a horse-riding nation, hence their full trousers and boots. Red boots are now often worn by folk-dance groups, but this is a modern innovation, black being more suitable to the military environment from which the costume developed. A black felt hat with a shallow brim is popular in many regions.

In the region of the Tatra mountains in the south the costume varies a great deal from the rest of the country. The women wear green or tan coloured skirts which are covered with floral patterns. A tight-fitting sleeveless embroidered velvet bodice, laced up in the front, has a basque at the waist. A white, long-sleeved blouse is worn with rows of multicoloured beads. The stockings are white and the leather *kierpce* are laced around the ankles. The hair is tied back with a ribbon.

The men wear thick white woollen trousers, which have black braid down the seams and across the back. On the front is a design in red, blue or black called *parzenica* and each mountaineer has his own design. A long-sleeved shirt is fastened at the neck and has a brass brooch on the chest. A very wide leather belt of about 25cm (10in), studded with brass studs and several buckles, is worn. A black felt hat has a band of white mussel shells and an eagle or falcon's feather on the side. A fur-lined white coat or cape is worn and is turned inside out in bad weather to protect the embroidery.

# HUNGARY

HUNGARIAN COSTUMES are among the most beautiful in Europe and are distinguished by their colours, the use of embroidery, very full skirts, layers of petticoats and the full, white, divided skirt type of trousers worn by the men.

Many of the women's skirts are of finely pleated cotton or linen, either plain or in floral designs. In the north region of Buják, a short pleated skirt is worn with eight or nine starched petticoats giving a very bulky effect. A round-necked, sleeveless bodice, made in a white material with a floral pattern, is worn over a white blouse which has gathered sleeves caught just above the elbow with ribbons. Several blouses have full pleated sleeves which are starched, thus giving them an exaggerated shape. A white apron embroidered with open-work stitching is very popular in Hungary. Married women wear their hair in a bun, tucked into little scarves or caps. A dozen or more rows of light-coloured beads are worn.

A costume derived from a wedding dress comes from the Matra Mountains region. A white pleated skirt is worn over several petticoats; the bodice is pale blue and a white shawl decorated with open-work embroidery crosses over and ties at the back. A white, tight-fitting, open-work cap is embroidered or decorated with flowers and has a bunch of floral ribbons falling down the back. White stockings are usually worn with black shoes or boots.

In the west and south, very elaborate floral-patterned cotton skirts in various shades of green, blue and red cotton are worn. Over the skirts, which can be pleated or gathered, are equally elaborate floral aprons, ending in a deep fringe. Bands of embroidered braid decorate the skirt and aprons.

A fringed shawl in a coloured pattern is often worn over a white, short-sleeved blouse. In some regions the blouse is worn without the shawl and gathered into the neck with a coloured bow. In the south, a dark bodice, laced up the front, is worn over the blouse.

The most elaborate and colourful costumes are from Mezökövesd, in the north-east, where the skirts are tightly fitting from the waist to the hip. Then, from a band of embroidery, the lower half is finely gathered. Around the hem of the skirt are several coloured bands of braid. Floral patterned materials, popular in so many Hungarian regions, are used for the skirts. A long black apron of silk or velvet reaches to the hem of the skirt and is embroidered with flowers and braid. A jacket with a high round neck has little gathered sleeves and a basque, which is fluted and covered with embroidery. White stockings with black shoes are worn. Unmarried girls have their hair in plaits, but married women have tight scarves round their heads, onto which are fastened large, white woollen pompoms.

HUNGARY. *The woman is wearing a costume from Kalocsa in the large central region called the Great Plains. This area is well known for its colourful costumes and wall painting. On the white walls of the houses, both inside and out, the women paint floral decorations. These beautiful designs are also incorporated onto the bodices, aprons and blouses of their costumes. The very full pleated skirt is worn with many* white petticoats. *The first petticoat is a short, tight one to prevent too much leg exposure when turning at speed during one of the popular* csárdás *dances. The man is wearing the pleated, linen trousers called* gatya, *which are found in many parts of Hungary. He is from the Transdanubia region in the west. The strong black boots enable him to execute all the* bokazo *clips found in the exciting Hungarian dances.*

At one time the wool was brushed so that it looked like hair that had been back-combed.

The men's costumes can be divided into two styles. In many regions tight black trousers are tucked into black boots and worn with white shirts. Occasionally the shirt is worn outside the trousers like a tunic. Black sleeveless waistcoats with one or two rows of silver or gold buttons are worn. In the winter, long-sleeved black jackets are very popular. In many areas black felt hats are worn; these can have black or braided bands around the crown or coloured ribbons with the ends hanging down the back.

The most popular and alternative costume is that consisting of a white linen divided skirt or trousers, called *gatya*. These reach to the calf and sometimes have a fringed edge. In Koppányszánto they are very full and gathered at the waist: in the west they are often very finely pleated. In some regions a black apron is worn, reaching to the edge of the trousers or skirt.

The most decorative costume comes from Mezőkövesd and is worn only on special occasions such as at the conclusion of harvesting. Full white *gatya* trousers are worn with black aprons that are heavily

*Man's sleeve from Mezőkövesd.*

embroidered and decorated with coloured braid. The shoulders, wide sleeves and front panels of the shirts are embroidered with flowers and braid. Black waistcoats are worn over the shirts and small-brimmed, high-domed hats are decorated with a broad black ribbon edged with yellow.

An interesting costume is worn by the shepherds and horsemen of the Hortobágy region. Here the linen *gatya* trousers are dyed a dark blue. A blue shirt with long wide sleeves has a turned-down collar. A black waistcoat with a round neck fastens with a row of silver or plain buttons. A black felt hat with a wide turned-up brim is worn; it also has a chin strap.

A large white or saffron-coloured felt coat, or *szur*, lined with sheep's wool, is worn like a cloak and the sleeves are sewn up and used only for decoration, or as pockets. These long coats, which reach to the calf, are decorated with braid and appliqué work. They are also made in sheepskin and are known as *suba*.

HUNGARY. *Both the man and woman come from the south-east part of Hungary. The woman wears a full pleated skirt in a floral design, typical of so many of the skirts worn in Hungary. Over the skirt is a large, floral apron. The neat green jacket is trimmed with lace. The jacket could be in various colours. Being unmarried, a bright colour is chosen. When she is married she will wear a special headscarf or bonnet. The man is wearing a shirt with full loose sleeves, a style which is found in many regions of Hungary. His black waistcoat-jacket has large silver buttons down the front, and the tight black trousers are tucked into his black leather boots. In many of the men's dances a feature is the* csapas *or hitting of the boots.*

# RUSSIA

THE COUNTRY that was previously called the USSR or Soviet Union covered one-sixth of the world's surface and comprised 15 major republics as well as numerous autonomous republics. Because of political changes the various republics have now become independent. Russia still remains the largest republic, but the name does not refer to what was once the whole of the Soviet Union.

There are many costumes in Russia, the most popular being the *sarafan* (illustrated), the straight *sarafan*, and the town costume of jacket and skirt. The straight *sarafan* is loose and flowing; it may be floor-length, ideal for the slow *khorovod* dances, or calf length, which is more suited to the quicker dances. The straight *sarafan* is the same pattern as the *sarafan* illustrated, but is not darted and fitted at the waist.

The town costume has a full skirt, long or short, some times with a frill around the bottom. It may be plain or floral-patterned.

The long-sleeved jacket is fastened up to the neck; it is always plain, not floral.

The colours that are mainly used for Russian costumes are red, pink, orange, yellow, green, cornflower blue or any bright colour, but not grey, brown, lilac or purple. The *kokoshnik*, or head-dress, may be in many forms. The very elaborate ones, covered in pearls and jewels, were only worn at grand court balls and functions. Headscarves are very popular. Red boots or shoes are worn with the *sarafans* and black ones are worn with the skirt and jacket.

A loose-fitting smock-type of shirt, the *rubashka*, is worn by the men. It is worn outside the trousers, with a red cord tied around the waist. Full sleeves are gathered into embroidered cuffs and there is a band of embroidery around the high, stand-up collar and down the shirt opening on the left side as well as along the hem. White or red is the most popular colour for these shirts. Black, slightly full trousers are tucked into black boots.

---

*RUSSIA AND UKRAINE. The woman on the left wears the very popular Russian* sarafan. *This fits into the waist and flares out into a full skirt. The dress can be made in a variety of colours and materials, either a brocade for a special occasion or in a softer material. Gold or coloured braiding runs down the front and along the top of the bodice. The white blouse has a round neckline and full three-quarter or full-length sleeves, which can be embroidered. The crown head-dress, or* kokoshnik *has a large bow at the back and the hair is dressed in a long pigtail. The couple on the right are from the Ukraine. The man wears very wide, full trousers*

tucked into red boots. His white shirt has embroidery down the front (Russian men have the opening on the left side). His wide sash is made in one long piece of cotton. This is wound around the waist, leaving two long ends hanging at either side. The woman wears a short skirt of woven material over a tight white petticoat that shows just below the skirt. The skirt has a design of squares, not checks. With no centre seam, its opening is covered by an embroidered apron. The korsétta or waistcoat-style jacket is velvet, decorated with a band of embroidery or braid. The floral head-dress of poppies, cornflowers and daisies has ribbons reaching down to the waist.

# UKRAINE

AFTER RUSSIA, THE UKRAINE is the second largest of the republics. The Ukrainians have a highly developed national sense, and this is shown in their songs, dances and costumes.

The women's costume is very attractive and highly individual. The very slim-line, tight skirt has a front opening, waist to hem, which is covered by an apron. This gap in the skirt allows the wearer to move quickly in popular dances such as the Hopak. The velvet *korsétta*, or waistcoat-jacket, may fasten down the front or on the side – as shown in the illustration.

Black, red, orange, cornflower blue or dark green are popular colours – never lilac, purple, grey, silver or gold.

The embroidery on the blouse, apron and petticoat is mainly in red, black and blue. The actual pattern differs according to the region. When the *korsétta* is not worn, a black or dark wrap-across skirt is then put on; the skirt crosses over the front and fastens on the left side. It is embroidered down the side and along the hem. A blue band is worn around the head and tied in a bow at the back. Red boots are usual.

# THE BALTIC REPUBLICS

## ESTONIA

Estonia, a land full of songs, dances and folklore, has some very colourful costumes. In common with other northern countries, stripes are very popular with either deep horizontal bands around the skirts or fine downward stripes. The skirts are woven in a heavy material and are gathered at the waist or have very fine tucks. Dark red is a popular colour, but they may be in black, yellow or orange.

Sleeveless bodices are worn with some costumes; these are decorated and fastened with silver rosette clips. A white, long-sleeved blouse is gathered into the cuffs and a wide, lace-edged collar is fastened with a brooch.

When a perpendicular-striped skirt is worn it is partnered with a heavy apron in the same shade. A black belt with a silver buckle holds the apron and skirt in place. No bodice is worn, but the blouse has red

LATVIA AND ESTONIA. The woman on the left is from Latvia, while the woman on the right wears a costume from Estonia. The Latvian costume has a very decorative bodice in an unusual design worked in silver braid. The full black skirt has a deep border of red, embroidered with old Nordic patterns. On the white blouse, the black embroidery is created with a very fine stitch and is shown on the shoulder seams, collar, neck opening and on the bottom edge of the sleeves. A decorated crown, not unlike those from Lithuania, is made in red, silver and gold. Large, antique, round silver ornaments are worn, very similar to those found in Norway and Finland. The woman from Estonia wears a heavy skirt and a bodice to match, made of the same woollen material. Silver buttons fasten the bodice up the front. The belt is hand-woven. White, striped or decorated stockings can be worn. The firm black leather shoe and the length of the skirt allow room to move in polkas and waltzes.

and blue embroidery along the top of the shoulders, around the collar and on the cuffs. A very tiny hat just sits on the top of the head. White stockings are usually worn, but there are also gaily coloured striped or patterned stockings to the knees. Black shoes sometimes have a decorated tongue over the instep. Some costumes have a loose pocket fixed on to a belt, as is found in Scandinavian countries.

The men wear black breeches, fastening at the knees with silver buttons, with a patterned or dark waistcoat, and a white, long-sleeved shirt fastened at the neck with a braided tie or brooch. A braided belt has two long ends and sometimes a skullcap is worn. Stockings are white, either plain or with a design, and the shoes are black.

## LATVIA

The costumes of Latvia, of which there are several, are very different from the neighbouring countries of Lithuania and Estonia. All three Baltic republics have different styles, although all have strong Nordic and Scandinavian similarities.

Skirts are long and in dark colours with a plain or decorated band at the hem. The bodices vary in style and shape. Unlike their Estonian neighbours, stripes are not used and the dark costume gives a very dignified look. In some areas a cream cloak is worn like the draped plaid of the Scots; it is fastened on the left shoulder with a round silver ornament.

Men wear long, calf-length white or cream coats that are embroidered down the front edge in black. Long white or cream trousers are gathered into white or coloured ankle bands. Shoes are black, the socks are white, while the white shirt has a turned-down collar with a knotted braid bow. A long braid belt is tied around the coat.

## LITHUANIA

Lithuania is one of the Baltic republics, sharing a border with Poland in the west and Latvia in the east. The Lithuanian women are very proud of their costumes and their sense of individuality.

The women's skirts are hand-woven, so there is a great variety in the designs. The aprons are also handmade, and change according to the wearer and her district; they range from being fairly simple to being quite elaborate. Blue is a very popular colour and red is used a great deal in the embroidery. The sleeveless jackets follow the same pattern and shape, but the woven material alters according to the wearer. Long braided belts are often worn, which are tied around the jacket waist. Children frequently wear their hair in two long pigtails.

The men wear either plain or striped trousers (as illustrated); pale blue, grey or white are popular colours. A sleeveless jacket is worn or, if preferred, a loose waistcoat reaching to the waist. The shirt has quite full sleeves with a decorated cuff. The special shoes are not always available, in which case a lightweight shoe is worn.

BELORUS AND LITHUANIA. *The woman on the right is from Belorus. The costumes from this republic are considered to be the most colourful of all the republics. Her full pleated skirt is made in a mixture of horizontal stripes. The white linen blouse has full sleeves ending in embroidered cuffs. The horizontal blocks of embroidery on the sleeve are in red geometrical designs. The sleeveless red jacket ends in squares, very similar to those found in Poland. The bright apron is decorated with lace. Several white petticoats are worn. The Polish-style laced-up ankle boots are black, but red and dark brown are also popular.*

*These bright costumes reflect the lively dances of this region. The couple are from the Baltic republic of Lithuania. The woman wears a long, hand-woven skirt in horizontal bands and stripes with a sleeveless jacket. Aprons are varied in design but she has chosen a pale-blue background with red and blue embroidery and a red fringe. Her crown is decorated with blue and red braid. The man wears striped trousers tucked into the top of his decorated socks. These striped trousers are very similar to those worn in Poland. His sleeveless jacket is worn over a white shirt and his tie is braided, as is his belt.*

## BELORUS

The republic of Belorus was previously known as Byelorussia. It is situated between the Baltic republics in the north, Poland in the west, Russia in the east and the Ukraine in the south. The costumes and dances all reflect the influence of Belorus's neighbours.

The women wear white full-sleeved blouses decorated with horizontal bands of embroidery. The skirts are full and pleated in bright horizontal stripes in a mixture of red, blue, white, yellow, orange and black. The white apron also has horizontal stripes. The small black or brown bootees are very similar to those worn in Poland.

The men wear a white shirt with full sleeves and cuffs; the stand-up collar, front centre-panels, edges and cuffs are all embroidered with a red geometrical design. The shirt is worn outside the trousers, which are fairly full and in stripes of red, brown, black or green. The trousers are tucked into black or brown boots and a narrow red sash is tied around the waist.

# MOLDOVA

MOLDOVA IS ONE OF THE smallest republics, and used to be known as Moldavia. The countryside is very green and fertile, and the Moldovans' love of colour and embroidery is shown in their costumes.

The women's costumes have several variations. The full skirt can be white, red or black, and pleated; it has a deep embroidered band at the hem. Two aprons are often worn, front and back; these are woven in bright horizontal stripes, a style that is also popular in Romania. A white linen, long-sleeved blouse has a block of red and blue embroidery across the upper sleeve or lines of embroidery down the sleeves. Short white bolero jackets have embroidery on the neck, armholes and the lower edge and sometimes beads are used for decoration. A white or red handkerchief is tied at the back of the head or a posy of flowers at the side. Several petticoats, pale stockings, red or black boots, low-heeled shoes or laced-up Romanian-style sandals are worn.

Men have white or black trousers tucked into black boots. A white shirt is worn outside the trousers and this has red or blue embroidery around the neck, down the front and on the edge of the long loose sleeves. A red sash with two loose ends on either side or a broad leather belt is worn around the waist. A heavily embroidered white or black leather sleeveless jacket is worn. A black or grey astrakhan hat is worn on the head.

MOLDOVA AND GEORGIA (CAUCASUS). *The woman on the left comes from Moldova and her costume has strong similarities to those in Romania (at one time Moldova was part of Romania). Her pleated skirt is worn with two aprons, front and back. The tight-fitting black bodice is worn over a white blouse with full sleeves. The blouse has a simple embroidered design on the sleeves but this can be more elaborate. The design, as in Romania, goes down the sleeve rather than across, as in the Ukraine. Boots, red or black shoes, or sometimes small black ankle boots are worn. The Georgian woman from the Caucasus (on the right) wears a long, flowing costume in pale blue. Over the dress is a type of coat-dress that opens down the front and is made in chiffon or very soft, fine net. Very important is the stiff underskirt that allows the dress to stand out and away from the legs and feet; in the gliding dances, no movement of the feet should be seen. The hair is dressed in two long plaits, and the pill-box hat has a short veil attached to it.*

# GEORGIA (CAUCASUS)

THE CAUCASUS is situated between the Black Sea and the Caspian Sea. It comprises Georgia, Armenia, Azerbaijan, Dagestan, Adjar and Kalmuk. The Georgians shown an Asian influence in their costumes, especially in those of the women. The costumes are made of soft materials such as silk, satin and chiffon, all in subtle shades.

Skirts are long and full, and worn over equally long petticoats. The tops of the bodice or dress are tight-fitting with long, tight sleeves and a high neckline. Some of the dresses have tight sleeves to the elbows and then long, flowing chiffon falling to below the hands. Long white veils fall from a round pill-box hat, or a long scarf is crossed over the neck with the ends falling down the back. Small silver belts are worn or occasionally a brocade belt in muted colours, which has long ends falling down the front. The hair is dressed in two long plaits that fall down the front of the dress.

White or silver shoes with small heels are worn.

Men's costumes present a complete contrast. They wear tight-fitting black trousers, worn with soft, pliable black leather, heel-less boots, which are pulled on to fit rather like gloves. A white shirt is worn outside the trousers and is belted at the waist with a cord. The tight sleeves reach to the wrists and a tight band fits around the neck. A long Cossack-style coat reaches to the knees and has narrow pockets for bullets on each side of the chest. The long sleeves of this coat completely cover the hands but they are usually rolled back to reveal the shirt. The trousers are usually black, the coat red, brown, grey or white and the shirt black or white. A narrow belt is worn over the jacket and into this is fixed a dagger, often of great antiquity, and which has been passed down from one generation to another. A black or grey astrakhan hat is worn.

# The Central Asian Republics

## Uzbekistan

Uzbekistan is the famed land of the 'Golden Road to Samarkand'. The original inhabitants of the Asiatic republics were Moslems and the Islamic background is shown in the style of dress. Cotton is used extensively for clothing in Uzbekistan and the designs show a blending of colours in stripes of multicoloured patterns. As in many Asiatic countries, women wear trousers under their dresses or tunics. One of the most popular of the Uzbek women's costumes is the calf-length dress, which has a turned-up collar and wide loose sleeves reaching to the wrists. The cotton trousers are white or in plain colours blending with the patterned dress and gathered into narrow bands. The black hair is dressed in several long, tiny plaits, the number marking the degree of beauty. A velvet, embroidered skullcap or *tyubetevka* is worn both by men and women; it has a tassel for festive occasions. Coloured shoes that have low heels are worn.

The men wear loose-fitting cotton coats called *khalats*. These are long sleeved, knee length, and with a coloured handkerchief tied around the waist. They are made in various coloured stripes. A white shirt is worn under the coat and dark-coloured trousers are tucked into black boots.

## Turkmenia

The famous Karakul sheep are bred in Turkmenia and their grey, black or brown wool is used extensively in the making of costumes.

The women wear very colourful loose caftans with long contrasting trousers that end in decorated bands. The caftan has a centre opening from the round neckline to above the waist; the small stand-up collar and the front opening are decorated with braid or embroidery. The long sleeves are fairly full and gathered in at the wrist. There are various forms of head-gear; a coloured scarf tied at the back of the head is very popular. Cotton or heavy silk are used in the summer and fine wool in the winter.

Men wear tight-fitting black or brown trousers tucked into high black boots. A dark-coloured, long-sleeved shirt in grey, brown or black is usual, although a white or red shirt is sometimes worn. Shirts have round necks with an opening on the right side, and are embroidered. The shirt is worn outside the trousers and a brightly coloured sash is worn with it.

A very large, sheepskin hat in white or brown is worn. Sometimes a loose, three-quarter-length coat, similar to the Uzbek *khalat*, in two-colour stripes is worn over the basic costume.

*UZBEKISTAN AND TURKMENIA. The woman on the left is from Uzbekistan and is wearing the well-known 'Khan-Atlas' dress so popular in this country. The dress can be worn loose without the waistcoat, with short sleeves or without the trousers. The special material is unique and is only made and worn in Uzebistan. It can be in a range of colours. The little round skullcap, the* tyubetevka, *is worn over her long black plaits. The woman from*

*Turkmenia wears a loose basic caftan, a garment that is worn in numerous countries. This caftan is for a special occasion as it is very elaborate and decorated. The loose-fitting, three-quarter-length coat is studded with metal discs. The hair is dressed in two long plaits and the little round hat has a dome ending in a metal point. The shoes are of soft leather with slightly turned-up toes and a low heel.*

# ROMANIA

THE COSTUMES AND EMBROIDERY found in Romania reflect the Roman or Italian outlook in the use of colour and decoration, with beads, spangles, metal and silk threads, which have been developed in the geometric patterns and love of embroidery. Parts of the costumes date from the time of the occupation by the Ottoman Empire.

The basic materials used for costumes are flax, hemp, wool and leather. The costumes underwent certain changes in the nineteenth century when cotton was imported on a large scale and was eventually produced in Romania. The growing of silkworms in the south-east region led to the introduction of silken tissues and thread, which were used for veils and embroidery.

Of all the Balkan countries, the Romanian costumes are the richest in embroidery and design. Although there are variations from region to region, the embroidery retains the same characteristics, using designs in geometric form. Each region has a local pattern, the colours depending on the vegetable dyes available. Red is very popular in the north as the colour is obtained from the madder root. The basic colours are red, black, dark brown, blue, yellow and certain shades of green and violet. In the agricultural areas the colours tend to be brighter, but in the mountain areas darker hues predominate,

such as dark red, and black with white. In all regions older people wear darker shades. In the southern Carpathians black and white embroidery is used extensively. The most widespread form of embroidery is the one-thread type, which demands very fine and careful needlework.

There are three main styles of women's costumes, which are associated with various regions. The main features of regional costumes remain the same but colours, embroidery and other details change. In Oltenia, south of the Carpathians, and in Transylvania in the north, the main feature is the double apron. Over a white linen or cotton full smock or a skirt and blouse, two aprons are worn, one at the front and the other at the back. The aprons can have horizontal stripes of red, dark blue and white or, as found in the south, geometric designs in shades of yellow and white on a dark background. The aprons are also woven using metal thread and embroidered with beads.

In Banat, in the south-west, the more primitive form of costume is worn. Over the basic white smock is an apron but at the back there is a small oblong second apron called an *opreg*. This little apron is woven in coloured patterns in wool, silk, cotton or metal

*Romanian double apron.*

111

ROMANIA. This couple wear costumes from Vlasca, near the capital city of Bucharest. The woman wears a white blouse; the embroidery on the front and sleeves of the blouse is very similar to that found in Moldova, the two countries having close links. The black pleated skirt, which is open at the front, reveals a red woven panel. Down the sides of the skirt are borders of heavy embroidery, and a woven belt is fastened around the waist. The hem of the petticoat is also embroidered and shows below the skirt sometimes, as in the Ukraine. The flowing veil is worn well off the face and denotes that she is unmarried. The man wears his loose-sleeved, white shirt outside his trousers. The hem and sleeves are trimmed with lace and fine embroidery. He wears a wide woven belt and a sheepskin jacket. The hat is made of black sheepskin in a style that is found in many regions and countries. He wears opanci shoes which at one time were worn by most Romanians, but now a black shoe is preferred.

threads. From the *opreg* hang long fringes of coloured wool called *chite*, which reach to the hem of the skirt. There are variations in the *opregs*, according to region, village and age.

The women's blouses are the most attractive features of the costumes throughout Romania. The upper part of the smock can form the blouse, or the skirts and blouses can be made separately. Sleeves are full and gathered into cuffs and the collarless neck is round. The blouse has bands of embroidery down the front, around the neck and cuffs, and down the sleeves as well as on the upper part of the sleeves.

Another interesting part of the costume is the long head veil, or *marama*; originally made from hemp or linen, these were later replaced by fine cotton or silk. The way of draping this veil indicates the age of the wearer. Married women wear the veil covering the head and crossed under the chin with one or both ends hanging down the back. Young girls wear the veil away from the face and draped down the back. In Oltenia the veils reach down to the level of the hem at the back.

Sheepskin jackets are popular in many regions and worn both by men and women, especially in winter. These are beautifully decorated and, again, the decoration varies according to the region. White stockings are usually worn with the leather-type sandal or *opanci*, although these are often now replaced by an ordinary black shoe.

Men's costumes can be divided into two styles, but with regional variations. The most popular form of dress, found in the south, east and north, consists of white trousers, which are calf length and tucked into black boots or reach to the ankle and are worn with the *opanci* sandals. A white shirt with long sleeves loose at the wrist is worn like a tunic over the trousers and a broad leather belt or brightly woven waistband fastens round the waist.

In some areas, however, the shirt is worn tucked into the trousers. In the Transylvania region in the north-west the costume reflects the Magyar influence, as shown in the full, white, loose trousers. Working clothes are simple and cut more loosely than those worn on more festive occasions. Summer trousers are usually made of cotton, but woollen trousers are worn in the winter. The long, tight-fitting trousers, when worn with a tucked-in shirt, display a design in the front made with black or blue braid; this trouser decoration recalls the influence of the Ottoman Empire. Shirts are embroidered on the edges of the sleeves, hems, shoulders and upper sleeves and on the shirt front and collar. The colours and the amount of design used vary considerably from region to region. In some areas red is used only for older men and yellow for the young. In Maramures a woven bag hangs on the right side by means of a braided strap across the shoulder. The men also wear little straw or round felt hats which are decorated with braid and have a feather on the side. A black sheepskin hat is very popular, being seen in many regions. The most spectacular hat comes from Bistrita-Nasavel and has a crown of peacock's feathers.

# FORMER YUGOSLAVIA

THE FORMER YUGOSLAVIA comprised six regions, now republics. Each country has its own highly individual costumes, music, dances and, in some cases, language. The different republics share borders with seven countries: Italy, Austria, Hungary, Romania, Bulgaria, Greece and Albania. The costumes and dances near the frontiers have strong similarities and links with their neighbours.

The early costume was based on a long, white smock for the woman, covered partly by an apron or sometimes an apron both back and front, worn with an over-dress or jacket.

The man had a similar smock or shirt with breeches and gaiters. This basic costume has changed only

*A Yugoslavian* opanci.

slightly and in some regions not at all. The Slavs are renowned for their skill in embroidery, used extensively in costume decoration. Designs are usually geometric or stem from Christian or Byzantine sources; red, together with black, predominates. Materials are wool, jute, flax and leather. Many costumes have coins hanging from chains worn around the neck and also fixed onto aprons, jackets and head-dresses. These coins represented the dowry of a daughter and in times of trouble were a very portable form of wealth.

## CROATIA

Croatia has a long, beautiful coastline that borders on the Adriatic Sea, and which includes the

CROATIA. *This couple are from the area south of the capital city, Zagreb. This region is particularly rich in embroidery. The woman's basic dress is in white cotton/linen over which is a long apron reaching to the hem. This costume has red embroidery on the full sleeves and the apron. In other towns, the embroidery is much more elaborate with the apron and sleeves covered with a floral pattern or in colourful squares. Red predominates but blue, yellow and green are used, especially in the floral and geometric designs. Both the skirt and apron are* usually finely pleated and the red design can be extended right around the skirt. She wears a woven, red belt and has several rows of red beads. The jacket is usually taken off when dancing one of the lively kolos of this region. An embroidered bonnet with a red ribbon at the back can be replaced by having the hair dressed in two long plaits tied at the end with red ribbons. The man wears a long white shirt that is decorated around the neck, cuffs and sleeves. His red jacket is edged in black and silver buttons. Both wear leather Croatian opancis.*

UNESCO World Heritage walled city of Dubrovnik. In the north, Croatia borders onto Hungary. The costumes throughout the country are diverse and numerous, and include some unusual ones such as those worn on the island of Susak. Here the colourful costume resembles a short ballet tutu and is worn with bright red tights. In Orebic, on the Pelješac Peninsula, the women dress in long sweeping skirts, wear little straw hats and carry fans, reminiscent of the time when this region held an important maritime position in the nineteenth century. It was here that many wealthy naval families lived and built grand houses.

Costumes on the Hungarian borders have full, white, short skirts decorated with open-work embroidery, colourful blouses with white frilled necks, floral-patterned shawls and aprons, striped stockings and decorated shoes . The men wear the Hungarian-style, white linen, full trousers, with a white shirt worn outside under a decorated sleeveless waistcoat. Black boots are worn.

On the Dalmatian coast the Italian influence is seen in the long pleated skirts, either in white or dark colours, which are worn with black or coloured aprons. Jackets have long sleeves and the white folded head-dresses are based on the Italian *tovaglia*.

In Krk, short black skirts with red-, yellow- and blue-coloured borders are worn with low-cut sleeveless bodices in red or black, coloured aprons and white, full-sleeves blouses. Red or white stockings are worn with coloured shoes. A white, folded *tovaglia* is worn with two ends falling down the back or golden ribbons

are draped on the head. Men wear long, black, baggy trousers reaching to the ankles, black sleeveless waistcoats or black jackets. Shirts are white with full sleeves, socks are white and black, and silver-buck-led shoes are worn. On the head is a fisherman's black woollen-type hat.

One of the most interesting costumes found in Croatia has an apron with an extended bib with both sections covered with coins. This is worn over a long-sleeved smock and a red, sleeveless coat. Decorated white stockings are worn with leather sandals, and red pill-box hats, plain or covered with coins, have white veils. The man's costume that accompanies this style has wide, dark-blue, baggy trousers fastened into red decorated gaiters. A broad sash is sometimes worn with a stud-ded leather belt and pistol. Plain, striped or patterned waistcoats, with or without sleeves and fastening on the side, are worn over white, long-sleeved shirts. A short bolero type of jacket, decorated with gold or coloured braid, is worn over the waist-coat. A round hat, adapted from the Turk-ish fez and which sometimes has a black fringed tassel, is worn. Soft leather slippers are usual.

## SERBIA

Like the region, the costumes of Serbia vary considerably. Those from Lesko-vac have black sleeveless bodices and skirts. Gold braid decorates the low, round front of the bodice as well as the hem of the skirt. The white under-dress has a high neckline with wide loose sleeves embroidered with open-work. The dress hangs well down below the

SERBIA. *Serbia has many varied costumes. This couple are from Sumadija, south of Belgrade. The woman's skirt is full and pleated, with a striped horizontal pattern of blues, yellow and black. The pleats are made by stitching each pleat, damping them and baking the skirt in a warm oven. In some costumes, the pleated skirt is folded and caught at the back to reveal an under-dress or petticoat. The red apron, in stripes and geometrical patterns, is worn with a red bodice and white blouse. A red ribbon is tied around the arm just above the elbow. Her hand-knitted decorative socks are worn with* opancis, *which have a turned-up toe. Each country has a different design of this particular footwear, but only in Serbia are the turned-up toes so pronounced. The man's costume is fairly typical of the male attire found in many regions. The jacket, waistcoat and trousers are made of woollen material. The trousers are tucked into very colourful socks, and he is also wearing the typical* opanci *shoes.*

skirt hem and has a border of lace. A long white scarf is draped around the head and neck. Coloured patterned socks and leather sandals with slightly turned-up toes are worn.

White skirts are worn with perpendicularly or horizontally striped aprons and a three-quarter-length sleeveless jacket. Embroidery can be simple or ornate with a predominance of geometric designs rather than floral ones. Red, dark blue, yellow, black and orange are used extensively. Decorated socks and sandals with very turned-up toes are worn.

The men have rather baggy trousers tucked into brightly patterned socks reaching to just below the knees. Short waistcoats and jackets, made in dark-brown woollen material, are worn. Wide belts of leather with handsome silver clasps are also worn. The white linen shirts have loose sleeves. Round black sheepskin hats and sandals with turned-up toes complete the costumes.

## MACEDONIA

The basic dress of the women is a long, white linen smock with loose or gathered sleeves ending in cuffs. A geometrical design is embroidered in black or red around the hem, sleeves and neck and this embroidery can vary from the very elaborate to the simple, according to the occasion. A three-quarter-length white jacket, which can have either long sleeves or be sleeveless, is elaborately decorated with embroidery and braid. The Macedonian costumes are heavily decorated, with a blending of reds, orange, yellow and black in both the embroidery and the weaving. The rather heavy red woven aprons end in a deep woollen fringe and across the front there is a chain with silver coins: similar chains are worn around the neck. Coins are sometimes used on the aprons as part of a design. A large belt fastened with an elaborate silver buckle is worn around the waist. Stockings are knitted in red, white and black patterns and are worn with soft leather sandals. The head-dress consists of a white cotton scarf or veil, draped over the head and falling down the back; the edge is often embroidered with silver coins fixed at the front.

In eastern Macedonia men wear a white shirt with sleeves reaching to the elbows. A gathered skirt reaches to just above the knees and a broad decorated belt is worn. Under the skirt, white linen or cotton trousers are tucked into knee-high socks. Patterns using dark-coloured wools such as deep plum, black or dark blue with a red star in a diamond design are displayed on these socks, which are worn with the traditional leather sandals. A sleeveless waistcoat, braided around the edges and in dark colours is favoured. A round black sheepskin hat or a draped and knotted white turban is worn. In the west, short- or long-sleeved, dark maroon waistcoats are worn with a black or brown short-sleeved over-jacket. A white shirt, leather sandals and a very small flat, round hat is worn.

MACEDONIA. *This couple are from Galicnik in western Macedonia, a country that is rich in costumes and also known for their elaborate embroidery and decoration. The woman wears a basic smock, over which a heavy apron and jacket are worn. Red is a very popular dye and predominates in many of the costumes and embroidery, the dye being obtained from madder. The very heavy striped apron has two layers of thick woollen fringing. The heavy belt is decorated with large silver buckles and silver coins are attached to it. The colourful red jacket has rows of silver and gold buttons. The knitted socks are made of a strong wool and incorporate a geometric design. The head-dress is of white cotton, the edge embroidered in a square design and with silver coins attached. The wearing of veils reflects the long years of the Turkish occupation when women had to cover their faces. The man wears cream, tight-fitting woollen trousers. The trouser seams, front and*

*hems have bands of black braid as decoration. The braid helped to strengthen the seams and reflects the very old custom of protecting oneself from bad spirits by covering any openings with embroidery or braid. His short jacket is worn over a long-sleeved under-jacket. The hat is of grey sheepskin or felt.*

# BULGARIA

THE WOMEN'S COSTUMES IN Bulgaria are based on three basic styles, which change considerably within the six regions of Šop, Severnjaško, Dobrudža, Trakija, Rhodope and Pirin. All the costumes, however, are made up of a smock or chemise over which are worn various types of aprons, a *sukman* or over-dress, and an open tunic-coat called a *saya*. Double aprons – one at the front and one at the back – may be embroidered, gathered or pleated, according to the area. Sometimes the back apron is pleated in red, as in north-west Bulgaria.

The *sukman* is a short-sleeved or sleeveless over-dress with a low V- or U-shaped neckline. This garment is worn in many parts of the country. In the west the *sukman* is knee length, in the central and south-east regions it reaches almost to the ankles and has a richly decorated border, and in the east a short-sleeved bodice and a gathered skirt is worn over it. The *saya* or open tunic-coat, most common in south-west Bulgaria, may have long or short sleeves, may be plain or striped, knee length or long and may be with or without an apron – there are numerous variations. Plain aprons are worn in Pirin, striped aprons in Šopluk and checked ones in Rhodope.

A narrow woven fabric belt or an ornamental leather belt with elaborate silver buckles is worn with all these costumes. Knitted patterned socks are also worn with *tservuli* (leather sandals) similar in style to the *opanci* of former Yugoslavia. Head-scarves are often worn, or perhaps a veil, or a head-band with the hair plaited into one long plait. The main materials used are hemp, flax, cotton, wool and goat hair, with locally produced silk used only for special costume decorations and embroidery.

Embroidery follows the traditional patterns of triangles, squares and diamonds; geometric forms are often used in the abstract portrayal of stars, plants, animals and human figures. There is a great variation in motifs and colours. Each group of costumes has variants according to the district, from which it is possible to identify region, village and even household.

Men's costumes have two main styles. The older style, which was first favoured in the north-east and then became popular in other regions, has white woollen, tight-fitting trousers reaching to the ankles. The trousers are decorated with black cord which not only reinforces the seams, but makes shaped patterns on the front. A white, long-sleeved shirt is worn under a sleeveless white or black jacket. In some regions a white, knee-length coat is worn, with or without sleeves. A patterned, chequered or striped waistband, or *tukanitsa*, is worn either over the long coat or under the short jacket. For a young man this is in dark red or blue and the older

BULGARIA. These two dancers are from the Šop region of western Bulgaria.
The woman is dressed in a sukman or over-dress. This is made of a woollen material and decorated with fine white braid. Underneath the sukman is a basic smock, a garment that is found throughout the Balkans. The hem of the smock shows just below the skirt and is embroidered in a red design. The sleeves and neckline are also embroidered in red and a touch of lace is added to the end of the sleeves. Like her partner, she is wearing leather tservuli. The man wears a pair of white, tight-fitting trousers decorated with black braid. His black, short-sleeved jacket is decorated with white braid and his white shirt embroided in a red geometric design. The broad sash is in a black and white pattern, but he could have chosen a plain red or white one. His hat is made of black sheepskin but can also be white.

121

men wear black or a dark colour. White socks and leather sandals are usual, with a round black sheepskin hat. When wearing the 'white' costume, or *belodrešnik* there is a variety of choice in the jacket preferred.

The alternative costume worn by the men, the 'black' costume or *chernodrešnik*, is more comfortable to wear. The trousers are full and baggy at the top and made in black, brown and occasionally blue woollen material. Black braid decorates the trousers in the same pattern as on the 'white' costume. Different types of long-sleeved

*Sheepskin hat worn in Eastern Europe.*

shirts are worn, ranging from plain white to embroidery on white or made in fine red and black stripes. A black sleeveless waistcoat is worn over the shirt and in winter or on festive occasions a sleeved jacket is worn, either inside or out of the waistband. Around the lower leg and over the trousers long strips of woollen or flaxen cloth are wrapped spirally. Alternatively, thick white knitted socks and long felt boots or leather sandals are worn. The men's costume is completed by black sheepskin hats.

# ALBANIA

THE COSTUMES OF ALBANIA are very individual although they show the influence of other countries in design. Wool, woven at home, was obtained from the mountain sheep and the more affluent costumes would be decorated with elaborate embroideries with braids of gold and silver thread and coloured silks.

Women's costumes are in two styles, those with trousers and those with skirts, but both have numerous variations. The trousers can be very full and gathered in at the ankles and the colours used are dark maroon, shades of pink, gold and many

other colours in cotton or satin. With them are worn long tight-fitting jackets or bodices made in dark-coloured materials, and covered with silver embroidery or gold braid. A high, round-necked white blouse has wide loose sleeves with a ribbon or braid tied around the arms just above the elbows. A sash or silver belt is worn round the waist. There are heel-less slippers with embroidered toes or plaited leather sandals. A round pill-box hat is worn at the back of the head or a coloured scarf with a pointed end which is tied at the back.

The men's costumes are also in two

ALBANIA. This couple from Albania wear two very striking costumes. The white, fairly tight smock that the woman is wearing is the basic garment of many of the Balkan costumes. Over the smock she wears a bright red-rust coloured apron. The apron is not tied around the waist but around the hips, and is edged with black lace or crochet work to give the apron weight. Her short, tight-fitting blue jacket is decorated and the long, coloured, hand-knitted socks are in an unusual but old geometric design. The scarf has been ingeniously draped and fastened over her red felt hat. The man comes from the north of Albania, where they are known as Ghegs. Those who live in the south are known as Tosks. He is wearing the tight black woollen trousers that form the basis of many Albanian costumes. In the winter months the trousers are black and in the summer they are white with black decoration. The sleeveless jacket can also be white with black decoration, or black. Knitted socks similar to his partner are worn. When indoors, the sandals are removed and a special over-sock is put on.

styles, those with trousers or, alternatively, a pleated skirt, or *foustanella*. The Ghegs wear white or black woollen trousers that fit tightly to the ankles; the seams are decorated with black braid. A white shirt with long sleeves, either loose or with cuffs is worn under a white and braided sleeveless waistcoat. Waistcoats vary between the villages. In Kukes, in the north-east, a rust-red waistcoat with dark-blue facings is worn with a broad-striped sash, rust-coloured socks and black leather sandals. In the south-east black baggy trousers are tucked into white felt gaiters and tied under the knees with black cord. The costume is completed with a red sash and a black jacket decorated with gold braid. Loose sleeves hang down the back. The unusual white shirt that is worn has a small round collar and wide loose sleeves reaching to the elbows, underneath which long tight sleeves reach to the wrists. Shoes

are black and edged with red. The most popular form of hat is the white felt fez.

The pleated white linen skirt, or *foustanella*, is less full than those worn in Greece and reaches to the knees. Long white woollen tight trousers are worn underneath this skirt. A plain white woollen sleeveless waistcoat edged with black braid is worn with a white, wide-sleeved shirt and a black-fringed coloured sash. Over this is a black jacket with loose hanging sleeves. The white shirt has sleeves gathered into cuffs, and black or light brown leather sandals with large black pompoms are worn. A white fez or a black forage-cap type of hat are the alternative head-gear.

Colours used throughout Albania are black, white and a particular shade of rust-red, as well as a range of pastels. Designs are geometric with zigzags, squares, triangles and an occasional floral pattern.

# GREECE

NEARLY HALF OF THE present-day population of Greece lives in rural areas. The people tend sheep and goats and the wool, spun and woven in the homes, is used for their costumes. In the Macedonia areas mulberry trees flourish and silk is produced. Flax is also grown and the linen used extensively in the making of costumes.

The costumes in the north-east have much in common with those of Bulgaria. Over a basic white smock or under-dress, a horizontally striped apron is worn, or a dark-blue or black tunic dress, or *sukman*, which has the embroidered edge of the smock showing below the hem. With these costumes is worn a long-sleeved jacket that fits into the waist and is decorated very simply with gold thread and fine braid. Silver belts, knitted socks, soft leather sandals and chains with coins worn across the jacket front are found in this area. Dark or patterned headscarves and Greek berets with long black tassels are worn. In the Epirus region the basic white smock or under-dress has wide sleeves which have ribbons or braid tied round the arms just above the elbows.

Plain aprons, worn on the hips rather than around the waist, are found in Pogoni, while patterned or striped aprons are worn in other areas. Long or short jackets, with or without sleeves, are also popular. White or gaily patterned knitted stockings are worn with simple black shoes or leather sandals with black pompoms on the toes. Silk or linen headscarves are either draped around the face or worn so that they fall down the back.

It is in the central and southern region that the very distinctive Greek style is seen. Here the long skirts echo the flowing robes of their ancestors and in these regions there is a wide range of colours and materials: silk, cotton or linen is often used. Colours are subtle shades of blue, red, green and yellow used in conjunction with gold and silver thread embroidery or fine braid. An apron is sometimes worn over these long skirts.

Long-sleeved, tight-fitting jackets worn over a blouse or dress are found in many regions. Colours and styles vary according to the region and sometimes they are made of velvet or wool and braided or embroidered in gold thread or silk. They can be fastened at the waist, forming a type of bodice, or worn loose.

Costumes from Attiki, Trikeri and Karagouna resemble those of ancient Greece in style. A long, ankle-length, full skirt has an over-dress or tunic reaching to the thighs or knees; it is either in white or a contrasting shade and is worn with a belt.

Men's costumes can be divided into two styles, those based on the baggy or long trousers and those on the white skirt or *foustanella*. The costumes are fairly simple and usually of dark colours, which highlight the striking dresses of the women.

Each region has a characteristic feature: in Thrace the men wear dark woollen trousers that are cut in a special way and called *poutouri*. It was from these trousers that the name of the costume – the *Poutouria* – was derived.

In Macedonia they wear the *panovraki*, or long under-trousers, which are covered by a skirt. These trousers are also found in other regions and are made in white cotton or wool and tucked into leggings or brightly coloured knitted socks. The baggy trousers or *vraka* are very popular on the islands.

Short bolero-style waistcoats, or *gileki*, are worn and these are plain for work and decorated with braid and embroidery for formal or festive wear. These waistcoats are usually sleeveless, but in some regions, as in the southern Peloponnese, they have loose sleeves that hang from the shoulders. Sleeves of shirts are open or gathered into cuffs. Coloured shirts are used for work, but white is the formal colour. Broad sashes are tied around the waist; in Macedonia a black sash is worn by older men and dark red by the younger men. A bridegroom will have a belt of coins around his sash.

Shoes with pompoms (*tsarouhia*) or boots are the most usual form of footwear. Black or black and white socks are exchanged for more brightly coloured ones on holiday occasions.

Round caps or hats are made from lambswool, velvet, felt and are often in black. A type of fez with a long tassel is also very popular.

*GREECE. The man is an evzone, a palace guard in Athens, and he is wearing a foustanella. The woman wears a costume called the Amalia; this is not an old one but was specially created in 1830 and named after Queen Amalia, and has now become traditional. The ankle-length skirt can be in a variety of colours, pastel shades being very popular. The velvet gold-embroidered jacket, which is worn over a blouse, can be simpler than the one that is shown. The red cap, known as a fesi or kalpaki, has a long silk tassel. Married women would have a slightly larger cap, which is worn folded back and in various styles. The evzone in his foustanella can be seen on duty in Athens, the capital city. The garment was first introduced into Greece by Albanian warriors and it was adopted by the Greek soldiers as it gave them more freedom of movement. It is made from numerous panels of white linen, gathered onto a wide band.*

# CRETE

THE COSTUMES OF CRETE denote past influences and the Cretans are a proud and defiant race although they still retain the characteristic friendliness of the Greeks. The men's costumes portray their background very strongly, with white Minoan boots (*stivalia*), Turkish baggy trousers (*vraka*) and rather severely cut jackets. Usually a dagger is thrust through a purple sash or *zounari* which is 8m (26½ ft) long. The picture shows a black costume, but a similar style is made in dark-blue wool with a sleeveless waistcoat, or *gileki*, cut with a diagonal fastening. The waistcoat is red and the shirt white.

The women's costume has full white trousers worn under a white cotton dress. Over this is worn an apron with an embroidered hem and a tight-fitting jacket. A red sash is tied around the waist with the long end falling to one side. A red hat of draped cotton and black leather shoes are worn.

# CYPRUS

COSTUMES ARE NOW ONLY SEEN in Cyprus on festive occasions. They are made of wool, silk, cotton and a blend of silk and cotton called *itare*. Silkworms are bred on the island and all the materials are woven in the homes; wool comes from the fat-tailed Cypriot sheep.

Two styles of dress are popular: the *Karpasitiko* costume has a white, long-sleeved dress which is calf length with a high round neck. Under the dress are worn full white trousers, which can be embroidered or plain. A tight-fitting, long coat has loose sleeves and turned-back cuffs, which are decorated. The front of the coat is low cut and shows the dress. The coat can be made from a range of materials and colours. A white or coloured handkerchief is worn, draped or folded, on the head. This handkerchief can be embroidered or have a lace edging; geometrical designs and patterns are very popular.

The other form of dress is a black velvet, long-sleeved jacket worn with a long silk or cotton skirt. The skirt can be in plain colours or white, stripes – which are

CYPRUS AND CRETE. *The woman on the right is from the island of Cyprus and the couple on the left are from Crete. The costume worn by the Cypriot woman has strong links with mainland Greece. The long, full skirt can be in a variety of colours, or in stripes and checks. The long-sleeved jacket is in black velvet and embroidered in gold, and is very similar to the* Amalia *costume in shape and design. The woman from Crete wears the full white trousers under a white cotton dress. A knife with a silver sheath is tucked into her red belt and this indicates that she is either engaged or married. The man wears the full, baggy trousers known as* vraka. *These are very popular in coastal areas, on the islands and other parts of Greece. In Crete the trousers are much fuller and tucked into white boots, very reminiscent of those worn by the Minoans as portrayed on ancient murals. Around his head he wears a handkerchief with a fringed edge.*

very popular – or checks. The bodice is decorated with gold or coloured braid. A red fez or white handkerchief are often worn on the head. Black low-heeled shoes are worn with both costumes.

The men's costumes have full, baggy black trousers, or *vraka*, tucked into black boots. A black sash is tied around the waist and a black embroidered or patterned sleeveless waistcoat is worn over a white, long-sleeved shirt. A little round black cap is worn on the back of the head.

The Turkish population, on festive occasions, wear the costumes seen on the mainland. Blue is a popular colour, while various shades of red are often seen. The red fez, draped turbans and loose jackets are still worn for work.

# TURKEY

A THIRD OF TURKEY'S POPULATION lives in the towns and cities and the remainder in rural communities, some of which are very remote. Folk customs are still observed and costumes maintained, as is evident at festivals or other celebrations. The costume materials are woven in the homes and the actions of weaving are often demonstrated in many of the folk dances. Materials are light in weight, mostly in cotton and silk with floral or striped patterns. Embroidery is not used extensively although it may be found occasionally on jackets and trousers.

Women's costumes are very decorative with the various articles of dress blending colours together, thus making the use of embroidery unnecessary. Shades of red are frequently incorporated into the costumes as this is traditionally regarded as a helpful protection against malign influences. Henna is also used for this purpose and

parts of the body are stained with it.

The basic costume has changed very little over the centuries and there is little variation between the regions. Very full and baggy trousers called *salvar* or *shalvar*, are worn by women in most areas. In the eastern region of Elazig they are worn with long-sleeved white blouses and sleeveless waistcoats. The waistcoats are usually in the same material and colour as the trousers. Around the waist is worn a coloured and fringed sash. The waistcoat is often replaced by a long-sleeved jacket of waist length and this can be in a similar or a contrasting colour. Those for special occasions are decorated with gold thread or braid on the cuffs, the edges and the back. Occasionally the side seams and the front of the trousers are similarly decorated.

Another type of costume worn a great deal is based on a coloured, long-sleeved

TURKEY. *These costumes come from the south and show the blending of colours and stripes so popular in this region. The woman's costume consists of several garments. First there is the floral patterned dress under which she is wearing the striped, baggy trousers called* shalvar *or* salvar. *Over the dress is a striped, long-sleeved coat. A large apron is then tied around the waist and a white scarf is draped around the head and neck. The turban-style head-dress is decorated with coins and chains. Her soft leather shoes, called* yemeni, *have slightly turned-up toes. The man wears baggy trousers, similar to those of the woman but in stronger material and usually in black or shades of blue. He has a brightly striped shirt and a broad sash with a turban-style head-dress. He is also wearing the popular* yemeni *shoes.*

dress reaching to the calf or ankle with the conventional trousers underneath, but there are many variations of this costume. In Gaziantep, in the south near the Syrian border, the skirt only reaches to the thigh and is white in colour. It is worn with a black, floral-patterned short jacket. In Irabazon, a northern region on the Black Sea, part of the skirt hem is lifted up and tucked into a belt.

Religion and custom decreed that no man or woman should allow any hair to be seen, so both sexes wore a form of head-dress. In all the costumes the only part of the body exposed were the hands. Until recently women covered their faces with veils, or draped scarves. The most popular form of head-dress is the round fez or pill-box-shaped hat with a veil or silk scarf draped over it. The ends of the scarf either hang down the back or fasten under the chin. Often the fez is decorated with gold and silver coins with chains across the forehead. When the fez is not worn, a long scarf is tied in various ways over the head.

There are three different styles of trousers for the men. The full baggy *salvar*, which are similar to those of the women, are usually in black or various shades of blue; brown or black trousers called *zivka* are also very common and these are tight-fitting below the knees, but have several extra folds in the upper part of the garment, especially at the back. The other form of trouser is based on the full *salvar*, but these end at the knees and the lower part of the legs are covered by gaiters. High-necked, white, long-sleeved shirts are usually worn with sleeveless waistcoats or short jackets. The jackets, called *cepken*, are sometimes embroidered or decorated with braid. Striped shirts are worn in some areas. A red felt fez is a popular form of head-dress around which is tied a turban. In some regions just the turban is worn and can be in one colour or multicoloured. A coloured scarf is sometimes tied and knotted around the head. Along the Black Sea coast a covering called a *baslik* is worn; this consists of a long, black scarf rolled

---

*TURKEY. The woman is wearing the very popular long-sleeved jacket or coat called an uç etek. The lower part of the jacket is in three panels, with one at the back and two in front. Under the jacket she is wearing the traditional full, baggy trousers. One of the front panels can be lifted and tucked into the belt or sash for working or dancing. She could also fold both the front panels and fasten the ends at the back. The choice of material is striped and can be in a variety of colours with the baggy* salvar *in a plain contrasting shade. Her head-dress is very simple and consists of a draped white scarf. She*

*is not wearing the traditional* yemeni *shoes but an ordinary outdoor working shoe. The man has a different style of* salvar *to the one in the previous illustration. The baggy upper part ends in a tight-fitting section rather like a gaiter, which is decorated with black braid. His short jacket has unusual open lower sleeves and is worn over a waistcoat which is made with a diagonal crossing. The very broad sash has a white – or sometimes decorated – handkerchief folded in a triangle and worn across the top. This is typical of the men from Balikesir. Around a felt hat is tied a colourful scarf.*

and knotted on the head in the style of a turban, but with the two ends hanging on either side like ears. Soft leather *yemeni* (sandals) in black or brown are worn, but in the east and on the Black Sea coast soft black calf boots are more usual. A very broad striped sash or waistband is worn, sometimes with a broad leather belt over the top of it. Into this belt various weapons are fixed.

One of the more unusual costumes comes from Bursa where the men dance the famous *kiliç kalkan,* or sword and shield dance, dressed in early Ottoman military costumes. Dark-blue trousers that look rather like shorts, a striped orange shirt and a short blue jacket with hanging sleeves are worn. A deep waistband and a striped turban which is wrapped around the fez complete the costume. The soft leather shoes have a criss-cross lacing and are worn over white knee-length stockings.

# IRAN

THERE ARE MANY ETHNIC GROUPS living in Iran, each having their own costumes, which are simple in design and are loosely cut to suit the warm climate.

Islamic laws require women to be veiled. In the more remote villages, the women wear the enveloping cloak called a *chador*. This is worn over the head, draped around the body and pulled across the face. In the south, along the Persian Gulf, and in some of the other areas of the country, a black face mask is worn.

Cotton and flax are mainly used for costumes, being grown in the coastal areas round the Caspian Sea. In the fertile valleys mulberry trees flourish and silk is produced, which is used in the making of costumes worn on special occasions. In the city of Yadz, a silk tissue known as *yasdi* is made.

The women's costume are very colourful and the Iranians have a particular love of flowers, with roses and carnations being grown extensively in some regions. Trousers are worn with most costumes and have a straight line.

The basic costume consists of a loose tunic with long sleeves worn over a very full skirt and trousers. These tunics vary in colour, length and design. In Gilan, a region in the north-west, a deep waistband in red and yellow stripes is worn over a red, hip-length tunic. The skirt is white with bands of red, blue, green and black around the hem. Worn with this costume

---

*IRAN. The man and the young girl are both from the nomadic, but very large, Kashgai tribe who inhabit the south. The girl is wearing a dress that is the basis of many Iranian costumes. The top part is a loose tunic which is open at the side-seams nearly to the waist. Under the tunic she wears a full-length skirt and, although not visible, a pair of trousers. The head and hair are always covered, either by a round, tight-fitting cap embroidered with beads or coins, or a turban. Over the cap she wears a long scarf crossing around her neck and hanging down the* back. *Most common is a very long, white or coloured scarf draped around the head. Older women wear black or dark colours. The man has a striped, calf-length coat which has loose sleeves. A wide sash is tied around the waist. The side of the coat is open, showing dark-coloured trousers. He also wears a white shirt reaching his hips. The hat is reminiscent of the style worn during the days of the Persian Empire. Light brown and made of thick felt, it can be worn in various ways; in winter the side of the flaps are lowered to protect the ears.*

are red trousers. From Luristan, near Teheran, the loose knee-length tunic is worn with matching trousers and no skirt. In the southern region of Bandar Abbas, on the Persian Gulf, the loose red or blue tunic reaches to the ankles. Over the tunic, a little striped cotton, sleeveless jacket is worn. A long headscarf passes around the neck, across the back and ties in the front around the waist. On the Pakistan border, the loose tunic has bands of coloured braid from the high, round neck down to the hem. The decoration varies according to the village. The trousers and tunic hem can also have bands of braid.

The men wear full, white, baggy *salvar* trousers over which is a white shirt; the sleeves and edges of the shirt are often edged with bands of red. A coloured waistcoat is worn and a white or yellow turban is worn on the head. Another costume is the caftan, reaching to the ankles with a broad coloured sash tied around the waist.

The Kurds maintain their tribal dress with great pride. The men wear short, thigh-length jackets, fastened to the neck or open down the front. Blue, with a very fine blue stripe, is a popular choice of colour or a blue material woven in small squares to give a quilted look. Kurdish men wear white shirts with very long sleeves, which are wrapped around the jacket cuffs or allowed to hang down.

The white or coloured turbans are fringed and tied in such a way that the fringe falls across the face, acting as a 'fly whisk'. Turbans are worn in many regions and are sometimes wound around a small type of fez with a corrugated pattern. Round felt skullcaps and hats are also worn. Shoes and sandals are made in canvas or lightweight soft leather.

# MOROCCO

THE MOUNTAINOUS TERRAIN of Morocco has restricted communication and there is a marked contrast in the clothes worn in the towns and the villages and between the Arabs and the Berbers.

The women in the cities wear the loose-fitting djellaba in white, grey or blue made in cotton or gaberdine. This garment reaches to the ankles and has a hood attached. Across the face a short black or white cotton veil is fastened; this practice is not always followed by the younger girls, however. An enveloping cloak, the *haik*, is also worn, often over European clothes. The *haik* is made in white or black cotton, wool or a mixture of cotton and silk. The draping of this cloak varies in different areas.

In Morocco the caftan is very popular and at one time worn by both men and women; now it is essentially a woman's garment. It is a long garment with wide and loose sleeves, fastened in the front with a row of small buttons which are usually made of silk braid. The caftan is worn over an undergarment of light material called a *quich* and this covers the loose, full trousers, or *seroval*, which reach to just below the knee.

The caftan is worn indoors, but is covered by a striped djellaba or white *haik* outdoors. The old style of very elaborate caftans in heavy brocade are now only worn by brides. Women wear backless babouche slippers of Moroccan leather embroidered and decorated in a variety of designs.

There are numerous forms of head-dresses, usually with a loose head covering that can be drawn across the face when required. The Berber women tend to cover their faces only in the towns or if they think they are being observed or photographed. Headwear ranges from simple straw hats to long white or black fringed scarves knotted at the back. In parts of the south a coloured scarf is tied around a little brocade cap, with a silver band of coins which cover the forehead.

The women near Telovet in the south wear skeins of twisted coloured wool, kept in place by silver clips and ornaments. The hair is often plaited and worn on the top of the head and married women or widows use henna as a hair dye. Handmade silver jewellery is worn by most Berber women and this usually represents the wealth of the family. The fibula pins are quite large and beautifully worked and are studded with stones. Very long and elaborate chains hang across the chest from each pin.

*Silver fibula pins, jewellery and head-dress from North Africa.*

137

Large amber and coloured beads, the size of eggs, are also much prized. Jewellery is worn as for special occasions such as weddings.

Men also wear the hooded djellaba, made in either cotton or wool, according to the season, and in a variety of colours, although white is the most popular. The djellaba is worn over European dress or an under-shirt with or without sleeves. The garment is made with two slits at the sides, which allows the hands access to the leather satchel or bag that hangs from a woollen cord across one shoulder. This bag is sometimes worn outside the djellaba.

In the north, striped djellabas are worn for special occasions and are made in heavy silk. In the south, the djellaba is replaced by a long loose shirt of blue cotton and is known as a *derraa*. On the front there is a big pocket, which is embroidered with a different design according to the Saharan region. With this costume the men wear a long white or blue scarf, called a *shesh*, around the head and neck as a protection against the sun or sandstorms. The men of the Rif mountains wear short djellabas with a wide leather belt around the waist.

In the famous market square of Jemaa el Fna in Marrakesh, it is possible to see a whole range of unusual costumes worn by various traders and entertainers. The Gnaouas entertain the crowds by dancing, and wear calf-length, long-sleeved white shirts which are belted at the waist. Loose, knee-length trousers are worn and round black hats are decorated with white cowrie shells and beads. Acrobats, who are dressed in coloured baggy trousers and white shirts, belong to the brotherhood of Sidi Ahmed ou Moussa, south of the Anti Atlas mountains.

---

*MOROCCO. The woman is a Berber from the Rif area of north Morocco, but Berbers also live in the south and in the mountain ranges. The man is a water vendor, and his type of costume can be seen in all the busy cities and markets. The woman is wearing a loose-fitting, white tunic that acts as the basic garment. Around her waist is tied a type of over-skirt in bright stripes. In the winter a long piece of woollen material, woven by the wearer, is worn like a cloak. Stripes are very popular and each tribe has has a different pattern and also slightly different ways of wearing them. A special pin called a* fibula *keeps the material in place. Her straw hat is decorated with black braid and is worn over a white scarf. Berber women love jewellery and she is wearing handmade silver bracelets on her ankles and wrists. The man wears a dark red loose-fitting djellaba over which he has several leather studded belts on which he hangs his brass cups. He is carrying a brass bell that he rings to attract the attention of customers. Over a white cap he has a large straw hat with a fringe around the edge. The hat helps to protect him against the sun and the fringe protects against flies.*

# ALGERIA

THE MOST POPULAR FORM OF DRESS in Algeria is the long cotton or gaberdine hooded djellaba in white, grey or blue, which is worn with a short veil across the face. Alternatively, there is a large enveloping cloak, or *haik*, in white or black cotton or wool, according to the season of the year. It is draped around the body, pulled over the head and can be drawn across the face. In the cities, European clothes are often worn under the *haik*. Caftans are worn indoors or under the djellaba or *haik* when outdoors.

Away from the capital, the costumes are based on the style known as *mellia*. This is a long length of material draped around the body and fastened on the shoulders with two fibula pins. A belt or sash is tied around the waist, giving a blouse effect to the upper part of the garment. The fibula pins vary in size. Some are very large and some are joined across the chest by silver chains; all are beautifully decorated. On festive occasions women from the mountain areas wear belts made of silver discs.

An under-dress of a contrasting colour or fine stripes will have a *mellia* draped over it and this is also a style favoured by the Berber mountain women. Many of the Berber tribes spend a nomadic existence and each tribe has a slightly different style of dress but they all share a love of colour,

---

*ALGERIA. The woman wears the loose-fitting djellaba, a basic costume worn in many North African countries. The man is from one of the nomadic Tuareg tribes. In hot weather the looseness of the djellaba helps to keep the wearer cool and enables air to circulate. The choice of pale colours, especially white, is important as they do not reflect the sun. She covers her head and face as is the custom and decreed by religion. The central Sahara Desert is the home of the nomadic Tuareg. It is here that the men are veiled and the women unveiled. At the end of boyhood, men are given the blue veil, the tagilmus or* taguelmost *which they wear for the rest of their lives. The* tagilmus *is a strip of indigo-blue cotton about 3m (10ft) in length. This is wound around the head in a special way, forming a turban. It covers the eyebrows and lower part of the face, but the lower folds over the mouth are loose and can be lifted for eating. The cotton material used for the garment is dyed indigo from plants found in the Sudan. The dye easily stains the body, so the Tuaregs have earned the name 'Blue Men'. Both men and women wear rather broad, open-toed sandals with thick rawhide soles, which give a firm grip on sand and are also a protection against scorpions and thorns.*

using blues, pinks, dark reds and purple.

Another style of dress is an ankle-length, loose cotton under-tunic which has a short *mellia* draped over it without a belt or sash. This can be in the same colour, in contrasting colours or floral patterns and can be edged with gold or coloured braid.

In the mountain regions during the winter months or at night in the desert a woollen or thick goat-hair cape is tied around the shoulders. This is known as a *hiyyak* or *hendira* and it is also a protection against the sirocco winds and the sudden sandstorms.

On festive occasions, the women of Kabylia, in the north, wear a white costume with an elaborately designed silver belt. On their heads they wear a diadem hung with silver discs and pendants set with coral and enamel, silver ornaments and jewellery being much prized. Berber women usually have a chain hung with various charms including the Hand of Fatma and square amulets. Little leather purses containing verses from the Koran are fastened onto a cord and they are worn around the neck.

Head-dresses vary from region to region and also among the tribes. Head-scarves are tied and knotted in numerous ways around the head like turbans, and under the turban there is sometimes a piece of material which protects the neck and also acts as a veil. This material can also be worn over the turban. Tight-fitting caps have draped scarves tied around them, often in a contrasting colour. The women of the Ouled Nail wear turbans hung with gold coins and chains. Bare feet or light sandals of soft leather or babouche slippers are worn.

The men's costume is of a similar style to those of neighbouring countries, with the long-sleeved cotton djellaba, or the winter version in wool, the thick hooded burnous cloak and loose under-trousers. Men favour white, blue, grey and beige in colours; white is popular as it does not absorb heat and blue is considered to act as an insect repellent.

# TUNISIA

OVER THE CENTURIES THE WAY of life and dress have changed very little for people in Tunisia, especially for those living inland or away from the coastal towns. Women cover their faces; this is done by draping over their heads and around the body an enveloping loose cotton type of cloak called a *safsari*, or *sifsari*, white in colour for the younger women and black for the older. In the villages the *safsari* may be of bright colours. This garment not only hides the face but acts as a protection from dust and dirt for the garments worn underneath. In the winter the cotton cloak is replaced by a woolen one, a *haik*, which is usually white or grey except in the south, where it is black with red fringes. Away from the towns or public places the *safsari* is replaced by a simple cotton head covering which is drawn across the face when necessary.

In many villages women wear a long skirt called a *futa*, which is tied around the waist. The material is often in stripes or checks and this skirt can either be worn with a coloured blouse or over the *mellia*. Some Bedouin women drape the *futa* skirt around them to combine an overall costume. Red is the predominant colour, especially among those living in the oases inland and in the olive groves of the east. Blue is popular and is used a great deal in North Africa as it reflects the sky and the sea. A bright yellow is favoured by the women of Zarzis in the south. The Bedouins and the townspeople prefer darker colours such as purple, maroon and blue. In the mountain region of the north-west a vivid purple is worn. Stripes in two colours are popular together with floral patterns and checks.

For special occasions silk is used for the *safsari* and, as the religious custom demands, the head is covered with a scarf tied around the head.

In the more remote regions and in the south, many of the inhabitants are of Berber extraction and cover the head with a loose, coloured scarf, around which is tied a piece of material similar to a turban in a strong contrasting shade. Straw hats are also worn and on the island of Djerba the straw crowns are made into a peak.

Men wear clothing similar to other North African and Arab countries: there are only slight variations and changes of name. The burnous is a type of cloak or cape made of a thick dark-brown wool or camel-hair. A hood is attached, which is pulled over the head during the winter and also gives protection against sand and wind. Also popular is a long woollen coat, open down the front, which is a substitute for the burnous and is called a *kachabia* or *kashabia*. It is often made in black or dark brown woollen material and is striped.

A similar loose-fitting coat, which opens only to the waist, is called a *kadroun*. For the winter months this is made in

brown or black wool, but for summer in white or striped cotton.

The red fez is worn mostly by the older generation, the younger men preferring the popular *chechias*, which is a tight-fitting round hat made in felt. White turbans are also worn, with an end draped across the neck, or straw hats with broad brims called 'sunshine' or *mudhala* hats. In the towns European-style shoes or backless slippers are preferred, but in the country areas many go barefooted.

*TUNISIA. The woman wears the popular* mellia *and the man is dressed in a summer* djebba. *The* mellia *consists of a long piece of cotton material, about 5m (6yd) long. The material is draped around the body and fastened on each shoulder with silver pins. A woven belt or sash is tied just below the waist. Under the* mellia *she has a patterned or white high-necked smock or slip, with either long or short sleeves. This garment is called a* suria *or* meriol. *The choice of colours and material can vary considerably with the under-smock being in a contrasting shade. A white scarf is tied around the head* and over this is a coloured scarf or band. The heavy jewellery and brooches are often passed down through the family. Fastened onto her head-dress are gold chains, in an elaborate decoration that is worn for festive occasions. The man wears clothing that is similar to other North African and Arab countries, with only slight variations. He wears the most popular basic garment, the* djellaba. *Over this can be worn a variety of coats; in summer a lightweight coat in a striped cotton, known as a* djebba *is worn, as shown here. Underneath the garments his trousers reach to the calf.*

# EGYPT

COSTUMES HAVE CHANGED slightly through the thousands of years of Egypt's history. The material is still woven on the old style looms: cotton, which is Egypt's major crop, is used extensively for costumes. The women wear a very simple loose dress which can either be gathered into a yoke or cut straight down without the gathers. The square or round neckline and front opening are decorated with embroidery, braid, beads or pearls, according to the occasion, or can be quite plain. A very elaborate wedding dress from the Siwa oasis in the Western Desert has buttons sewn on the front in a sun-ray pattern. Coloured thread is used in the design – symbolic of the ancient Egyptians' sun god, Amon Ra. Numerous necklaces, beads, chains, earrings and bracelets are worn, especially at festivities, together with anklets, a symbol of their bondage to the soil.

At one time women would wear an enveloping black taub similar to the cloaks worn in North Africa, which covered the figure from head to toe. If not barefooted, a light sandal is worn.

For men a loose-fitting, long-sleeved type of shirt known as the *galabia* was introduced with the coming of the Islamic religion. A white turban or a red fez is the most popular form of head-covering, or a tight-fitting skullcap. Western-style shoes are worn in the cities, but in the country it is a type of sandal or feet are bare.

EGYPT. *The man wears a cotton* galabia, *similar in style to the* djellaba *of North Africa. The woman wears a simple tunic-style dress. As in many hot countries, costumes for both men and women are loose-fitting. The woman is wearing a simple dress, which forms the pattern for numerous designs. Slightly full and loose trousers are worn under the dress and a long veil falls down the back. The veil is attached in front to a dark-coloured head-band which can be plain or decorated with gold coins. The hair can be plaited and fall each side of the face, but in the desert regions very elaborate hair styles are created and these are covered by a loose black veil. The man wears the typical loose-fitting, long-sleeved type of shirt known as the* galabia. *Made in cotton, this garment can be in any colour, striped or plain. A white cotton shirt can be worn underneath, together with white loose trousers. Usually the* galabia *is worn without a belt, but occasionally a red sash is tied around the waist. A white turban or a red fez is the most popular form of head covering or perhaps a tight-fitting skullcap. In the country either sandals are worn or people go barefoot.*

# THE LEBANON

ARTS AND CRAFTS IN THE LEBANON and the making of material has changed little through the centuries and still continues in the villages. Silk, cotton and wool is woven on hand looms and the dyes are obtained from local materials.

The songs, dances and costumes are divided into three main styles, Dabke, Bedouin and Andalusian. A similar pattern of dress is found within all of the Levant countries and the ethnic links have been maintained in spite of changing boundaries. The most typical of the Lebanese costume is the Dabke, a style not only worn for dancing, but seen in the villages.

The Bedouins are found both in the Lebanon and Syria and have their own distinctive costume. Women wear a long-sleeved, loose tunic dress reaching to the ankles; it can be plain or have a front panel decorated with gold braid. Red, black, blue and green are all popular colours for these dresses. A long black veil is worn over a red or black pill-box hat, or around the head and neck. Another style has a decorated head-band, which is tied over a long white veil that hangs loosely down the back.

The Andalusian women's costume, so named because of the strong Arab links with Spain, has loose-sleeved, knee-length jackets that open at the front and sides. Full baggy trousers are worn underneath, with a round-necked, long-sleeved blouse. The red pill-box hat also has a white veil. Colours vary; the jacket can be pink or dark blue, edged with gold braid and with a gold belt. Trousers are usually white or pale blue. With most costumes a low-heeled shoe is worn.

The Dabke men wear either very full, black, baggy trousers ending tightly at the knees, or full baggy trousers tucked into calf-length black leather boots. The Dabke are mountain people and there is a difference of dress between the north and the south. In the south a domed felt hat is worn with a white scarf tied round the edge and knotted at the side but, in the north, the domed hat is black and worn over a loosely draped black scarf. A white or red fez is also worn and, for working, a pull-on knitted hat with a crown ending in a little tassel is worn.

The Bedouin costume comprises the loose djellaba in black, blue, grey or striped cotton. A heavy, loose *abaya* is worn over the djellaba and the *keffiyeh* headscarf is kept in place by the black *agal* or head ropes. A flat lightweight sandal is worn.

The Andalusian costume for men consists of full, baggy trousers which are worn tucked into their boots, together with a high-necked, full-sleeved shirt and a short waistcoat.

THE LEBANON. *The most typical Lebanese costumes are those of the Dabke, shown here. The woman is dressed in a long-sleeved cotton dress which reaches to just below the knees. Bands of braid decorate the hem and sometimes a short-sleeved jacket, also braided, is worn over the dress. Blue, green, red and pink are the most popular colours, as well as floral patterns. Older women wear a much longer skirt. White trousers, ending in a frill, are always worn underneath the skirt. A coloured headscarf is tied around her head and knotted at the back. The Dabke man wears full, black, baggy trousers tucked into calf-length black leather boots. The sides of the trousers are often decorated but for work they would be plain, as illustrated. He is wearing a waistcoat but to be less formal he would just wear his shirt. A broad black sash is tied around his waist. Sometimes the sash is coloured or striped.*

# ETHIOPIA

ETHIOPIA IS A COUNTRY that is filled with different tribes and racial groups, and there is a great variety of costumes. The most popular form of garment is the *shamma*, which is worn by both men and women. This garment is a long length of material draped around the body; it is made of cotton, calico or muslin, usually white in colour, and can be quite plain or have a deep border woven in geometric designs in bright colours. Women wear the *shamma* over a long white cotton robe or dress with long sleeves. The hem of the dress sometimes has a woven border which matches that of the *shamma*. The way the *shamma* is draped can denote region, status and age. In the north the women tend either to drape a lightweight cotton *shamma* over their heads or let a corner fall down their back in a triangle which often reaches to the hem.

Some of the more elaborate town costumes of former years are not now seen, being replaced by the simple *shamma* and dresses. Occasionally more affluent women wear a long white robe of thick cotton with a narrow panel of multi-coloured embroidery down the front. White is the predominant colour as it does not absorb the heat.

The Ataya women wear a loose white cotton dress with a patterned border and dispense with the *shamma* as it would hide the amber beads, coloured stones and silver balls worn around the neck. They tie coloured scarves around their heads over felt skullcaps.

In the more primitive areas of the hot south-west, only a short type skirt is worn with an end draped over the shoulder. Sometimes the naked top of the body is decorated by the wearing of numerous

ETHIOPIA. *This couple are from the Aderi tribe and come from the walled city of Harar. The woman wears the very practical and adaptable* shamma, *which is a long length of material draped around the body (traditionally in a way that kept the left arm free). This acts as a protection against the weather, especially the hot sun. She wears a simple cotton dress underneath and goes barefooted. The man also wears a* shamma *but he has draped it over a white, long-sleeved tunic shirt. Both the shirt and his trousers are made of linen or cotton. He goes bareheaded and would wear loose, leather sandals if he was going into a town or city.*

ivory and coloured beads and there are also necklaces of hair made from the tails of giraffes. The lower lips of these women are pierced and from them hang bead necklaces. Bracelets, rings and ear clips are worn by many groups. Silver is the metal usually used although the richer town dwellers might have gold. Christians are identified as such by the wearing of a coloured band around the neck, called a *mateb*. Ornate crosses made in Coptic or Portuguese designs are also very popular.

The accepted dress for men is a white, long-sleeved tunic shirt worn outside long white trousers, made of linen or cotton. They also wear the *shamma*, sometimes with a woven border. It is draped in different ways according to the region, but the men usually have it over the right shoulder and the women over the left. The draping can also have special significance, such as when attending church, celebrations or visiting someone of high rank. On feast days, a tunic of striped silk is worn with the *shamma*.

The various hill and desert tribes wear loose, short trousers with shirts or a *shamma* draped around the body in various ways, either over the shirt or like a toga around the body. In rainy weather, townspeople, both men and women, wear a heavy felt cape which is conical in shape with openings for the arms and hands. Shepherds' capes are made from animal skins and the members of the church are distinguished by a black cape that hangs loosely from the shoulders.

Turbans are worn by many Ethiopians and these are rather high and round in shape; they are made of white cotton, though monks have yellow. Many of the tribes go bareheaded and specialize in elaborate plaited hair, formed into shapes using mud or melted butter. Both men and women go barefooted or in the towns wear loose sandals of leather or plaited grass.

# SAUDI ARABIA

THE COSTUMES WORN IN THE CITIES and towns of Saudi Arabia are similar to those found in other Arab countries. The women wear the long-sleeved, loose-fitting, ankle-length dresses in materials which range from printed cottons or silks to a mixture of both. Over the dress, (*thōb*, or *tobe*) is worn a large, black, flowing cloak which covers the dress, head and face. Loose-fitting trousers are worn under the *thōb*.

Among the Arabs, both men and women keep both the body and the head well covered. A woman never appears in the streets unveiled and even in her own home the veil is only removed in the presence of her closest relatives and never if men are present. The older women are not required to be so strict, but the custom has become habitual. Younger girls under the age of nine may go unveiled and women may relax the rule of being veiled in the presence of very young boys and very old men. A black face mask often replaces the veil, which allows full use of the hands.

The man's costume is also based on the *thōb* or *tobe*. A loose-sleeved coat, called a *gumbāz* or *kibber*, is worn over the *thōb*. A large sleeveless cloak called an *abāyeh* is also worn. This can be made from cotton, fine wool or a coarse wool which is woven in stripes or can also be made in a material that is based on silk with embroidery around the neck and front edges.

The nomadic tribal groups known as the Bedouin also live in Saudi Arabia. Each tribal group has a slightly different costume which indicates locality, social position and marital status; these are revealed by the embroidery on the women's costume, the head-dress and hair style, the jewellery and the pattern or colour of the material that is used. Red embroidery is only worn by married women and blue by young unmarried girls. The loose *thōb*, or dress, is usually black or blue and highlighted by embroidery on the neckline, sleeves and hem, but these are not for everyday use and the working costume is very plain.

Married women wear a head veil over which is a turban or band that may be decorated with silver coins. Alternatively a head veil or cloak is worn over a turban.

The Bedouin men are less distinctive in their costume and wear the typical Arab *thōb*, *gumbāz* and *abāyeh*. The *keffiyeh* is often draped under the chin and can be lifted across the face as a protection against sandstorms. In the winter it is crossed under the chin and fixed on top of the head to give warmth.

Women will often be barefooted or wear sandals. However, the men, when not barefoot, wear either a Western-style shoe, ankle boot or sandal.

# IRAQ

THE COSTUMES OF IRAQ follow a pattern similar to those worn in other Arab countries but with differences in names and styles. In the central and southern regions there is very little change, but the northern tribes of the Kurdish, Turkmen and other smaller groups wear a very distinctive form of dress.

In the ancient capital of Baghdad and the surrounding areas, the women wear a loose tunic dress with long sleeves, not unlike the djellaba, which is called a *hashimi*. Made in cotton or a blend of cotton and silk, and in various colours, black and green predominate. A floral pattern or geometric design is often woven into the material. As is the custom with Arab women under the Moslem rule, the head and face are covered with a large black cloak or *abaya*. The cloak is held loosely around the body, enveloping the *hashimi*, and drawn across the face. Made from a light material, it can also be in fine wool.

The women in the south and central regions wear a *hashimi*, often decorated around the neck and down the front and sleeve edges. Blue is popular, with white, gold or variously coloured embroidery or braid. Silver or gold bracelets, earrings, anklets, nose rings and rows of coloured beads are worn extensively in this region.

The full, black *abaya* cloak, first worn when a girl comes of age, is an essential part of the costume. Women wear ankle-length full trousers under the *hashimi*. Shoes are of soft leather and made like a backless slipper or moccasin. The face, neck and body are often tattooed.

Men also have an established style of dress; the loose robes are as they have been worn for many centuries. In Baghdad and the surrounding areas a long, white shirt, buttoning from the neck to the waist, and reaching to the ankles, is worn; this is known as a *dishdasha*. Over this garment is worn a long, cross-over coat called a *zaboon* or *saya*, which is made in striped or plain-coloured materials. Trousers, or *sherwal*, are of white cotton and the backless shoes or sandals are of leather.

Over these basic garments a large *abaya* is worn. Made from camel hair, it is in white, brown or black and can be plain or decorated with braid down the front and on the sleeve opening; this decoration is often very elaborate. A turban or wrapped scarf, known as a *jarrawiyah*, is the traditional head-dress of this region.

Colours vary but white, beige or a striped material are worn a great deal. A draped white headscarf, or *kuffiya*, is worn over a white skullcap and is kept in place by a cord, or *iqal*, made of camel hair. This cord can be knotted in various ways and can be in one or two thicknesses. The headscarf can also be in checked cotton of red and white or black and white and is known as a *yatshmagh*. Different types of

SAUDI ARABIA AND IRAQ. *The child and her father are from Saudi Arabia; the Kurdish man on the right is from northern Iraq. The little girl wears a loose-fitting dress and over her head and around the top of her body she has a black, flowing cloak. Being very young, her dress can be short but soon the dress will have to reach to the ankles and she will also have to wear trousers – a strict code of dress is adhered to. Her father wears the typical Arab dress of a long, white tunic/shirt, a* thōb *or* tobe, *which reaches to the ground. Under this he wears*

*calf-length white trousers. The* thōb *is made of cotton or fine linen and can be white, blue, grey or beige. Over this basic garment he has a loose-sleeved coat, the* gumbaz *or* kibber. *A white, knitted skullcap covers the head and over this is worn a head-veil, the* keffiyeh. *The* agāl *(head-ropes) keep the scarf in place. The Kurdish man is dressed in summer clothes made from a coarse cotton. His felt hat has a scarf wrapped around it. The feather tucked into the hat is a sign that it is a festive occasion.*

scarves denote region, profession and tribe. The footwear and trousers worn are similar to those found in Baghdad.

The Kurdish people in the north have many different styles, according to the tribe. The women's costume is based on the long, loose *hashimi*, made in coloured cottons in stripes and worn with or without a belt or sash. A scarf is draped around the head and face over which is placed a coloured turban. The turban can be fringed or hung with jewellery and coins. There are many different styles of head-dresses.

Men wear a loose, long-sleeved jacket over a shirt. A broad sash is tied over full and baggy trousers. These trousers and jackets can be white, black, blue or striped. The turban is tied with a fringed edge. Lightweight leather moccasins or sandals are worn.

# ISRAEL

ISRAEL IS A COUNTRY that is now both old and new. Jews came from many countries to settle in Israel and each group brought with them different ethnic cultures that blended with the ancient traditions. Also living in the country are Arabs and Druzes.

Jewish communities throughout the world have always worn a very distinctive form of dress and over 300 different costumes are housed in the Haaretz Museum in Tel Aviv. However, they are an inheritance from particular groups and countries and are not really representative of the new nation. A costume was therefore evolved to suit the folk culture that developed and folk groups which represent Israel wear either the old or the new.

The old style is shown in the Yemenite costume based on those worn by the Jews who returned to Israel from the Yemen. This costume is typical of a desert community and has only changed slightly through the years.

The women wear a calf-length, loose, black tunic, which has long sleeves and a high neckline. A decorated and embroidered panel extends down the front. Black cotton trousers are worn under the tunic and the head-dress consists of a tightly

*Yemeni head-dress.*

155

fitting black hood, which has a rich decoration of braid and gold coins. Alternatively a loose white or coloured headscarf is worn over a band or other coloured scarf already tied around the head.

The men wear a loose, white cotton, calf-length tunic with a broad belt around the waist and a white turban on the head. Both men and women go either barefooted or wear light sandals. There are many variations of these costumes.

The Arabs wear their traditional garments. A shepherd has a white cotton shirt, or *galabia*, fastened around the waist with a leather belt. A black *abaya* coat of camel hair or wool is worn for warmth and on his head a white scarf is held in place with black cord. The scarf can be loose or tied in turban fashion. Women wear a loose black tunic style of dress, often with a band of material tied as a belt. A square panel of embroidery is at the neck and a white scarf covers the head. Black trousers are worn under the tunic and, when not barefooted, a light sandal is worn.

*ISRAEL. This couple wear modern costumes used for dancing; these were evolved to represent the new State of Israel. The women's costume is simple in design and gives plenty of freedom to move when dancing the fast Israeli horas, or the slow fluid dances. There is no set design. Each group creates their own costumes, but all are based on a short, knee-length, full-skirted dress that has wide loose sleeves. Coloured braid or contrasting material decorates the dress in a variety of ways, according to the dance group. The braid can be around the hem of the skirt and sleeves, on the neckline or down the front. The man wears a loose shirt, worn outside the trousers. Like his partner's costume, the design and colours of the shirt and trousers can change. No head-dress is worn and the dancers usually perform barefooted.*

*SRI LANKA. This couple are dancers from Kandy, a famous place of pilgrimage for Buddhists. The dances are mainly for men but women do now take part and wear the counterpart to the man's costume. Fine cotton material is gathered into a waistband and held in place by the heavy ornamental belt, and she wears a loose draped* dhoti *below two layers of braided outerskirts. The man wears white cotton trousers under his gathered skirt; they are tight-fitting around his ankles and lower calves and loose above. The breastplate is made of braid, silver discs and beads – the pattern can vary with each dancer. The head-dress is also made of silver and studded with gems.*

# Sri Lanka

THE COSTUMES WORN throughout the island of Sri Lanka are very simple in design. Women wear either a cotton wrap-over sarong or a sari. The sarong reaches from the waist to the ankle and is worn with a tight-fitting, short-sleeved blouse. The sari is a long length of material gathered into the waist with one end draped over the left shoulder of the blouse. Colours vary considerably; the sarong and blouse can be white or the two garments can be in contrasting colours. Pinks, blues and pastel shades are very popular. No hats or head-dresses are worn but, when necessary, the sari is draped over the head. The tea plantation workers often cover their heads with a wide white headscarf as protection against the sun and this helps to support the straps of the collecting baskets on the backs, the straps passing across the head.

Men also wear the cotton sarong, with or without a loose white shirt, according to the occupation of the wearer. White is worn a great deal and the men also favour checks for the sarong, although colours are seldom strong or violent. No head covering is worn and both men and women go either barefoot or wear a light sandal.

# India

INDIA'S ARTISTIC TRADITIONS, which are deeply rooted in religion, greatly influenced music, customs, dance, festivals and associated costume.

The most popular form of dress for women is the sari, which can be made in a variety of materials, from cotton to silk. Indian cotton has been made for thousands of years and is the most popular of materials used today. Patterns, colours and fabrics vary according to the regions: colours are obtained from vegetable and mineral dyes and are strong in tone. The border of the sari and the final metre is decorated in patterns, mostly based on living forms. The elephant, peacock, lotus, mango, buffalo and various trees are some of the shapes that are incorporated into patterns. Some of the most elaborate patterns are made in gold, so that when the sari is finished with it is burnt and the metal recovered.

Varanasi is well known for its fine silk saris with the borders often brocaded in silver and gold. Kashmir weaves saris in the famous designs that influenced the Scottish paisley shawls of the nineteenth century. Pochampalli silk saris have the whole material covered with ancient patterns. From Sanganer, hand-blocked printed muslin saris are made: from Chanderi there are the cotton saris. A very light silk sari is made in Tassar, which is woven from the cocoon of the wild silk moth.

In the south the sari can be worn in a *coorgi* style with the pleats at the back. When working on the land, the sari is pulled through the legs to form a type of trouser and the *pallu* is draped over the right shoulder.

Brides wear a very elaborate sari, usually in red and with a green *choli*. Draped over their head is a long piece of red material, or *chuni*, which is decorated.

In some of the northern regions, very full skirts called *ghagra* are worn with a *choli* and a long length of material like a stole, known as a *dupatta*, is wrapped around the head and shoulders. In Kashmir and the Punjab, coloured loose tunics are worn over trousers. This type of costume can replace the sari and is worn mainly by the Moslems both in India and Pakistan. The knee-length tunic, called a *kameez*, or a slightly looser style known as a *kurta*, are both worn over *salwar* (trousers). The trousers are often gathered in at the ankles and are popular with young girls.

The men's costume is based on the *dhoti*, a length of material in cotton or silk printed with or without a border. This is tied or wrapped around the lower part of the body in numerous ways, according to the region. When men work on the land it can be pulled through the legs and tied to form a loose trouser. A shirt or loose tunic covers the upper body or just a long *dupatta* is worn, wrapped around the shoulders and chest. The Punjabi men wear white shirts over a coloured dhoti, a black sleeveless waistcoat and an elaborate turban. Around the neck is a string of yellow beads. Turbans are worn in many regions. Muslim men wear a dark round hat and, on special occasions, little boys wear velvet ones decorated with braid and beads. Throughout India both men and women are generally either barefooted or wear open sandals.

In complete contrast are the costumes worn by the classical dancers. Religious in inspiration, the best known style of the dancing is that of the Bharat Natyam, which comes from the south of India. *Kathakali*, an ancient dance from Kerala, has the most elaborate of all costumes.

---

*INDIA. The woman is dressed in the popular sari and the man is a Sikh from northern India. The sari can be worn in numerous ways depending upon the province. The garment consists of a length of material, 5–9m (16½ –30ft) in length and 105cm (42in) in width. The material can be cotton, muslin, silk or nylon. It may be simple in pattern or very elaborate, depending on the occasion. The range of colours and choice of design is vast. The sari is worn over a tight-fitting, half-sleeved or sleeveless bodice called a choli. A long petticoat is worn which reaches to the ankles and is tied at the waist with a drawstring. The sari is wrapped around the petticoat, pleated in front and tucked into the top. The long end, the pallu, is draped over the left shoulder. The pallu can also be draped over the head or tucked into the left side of the waist to form a drape. The man, who is a Sikh, wears a button-through, knee-length jacket or shirwani with tight, white trousers, or churidar. He wears a white turban in order to cover his hair which, for religious reasons, is kept long and must never be cut.*

INDIA. *The couple are two dancers, performing the classical Bharata Natyam from Southern India. The woman is wearing a costume that was created when Bharata Natyam became a part of theatre performances. The skirt is made rather like draped trousers with the fan-pleated piece in front. A separate piece is worn around the hips. The bodice is the traditional* choli. *The various items of jewellery are an essential part of the costume. Made of gold, they are set with rubies, small gems and pearls. The pendant, the* tika, *worn on the forehead, covers the hair parting and is attached to a string of pearls and gems. On either side of the* tika, *and fixed into the hair, are two clips. The one on the right side is round and represents the sun; the one on the left side is shaped like a moon. Armlets and bracelets decorate the arms. Dancers have their hair drawn back into a long plait that is covered with a hooded serpent ornament or* jadai naga, *which is a symbol of space and eternity. The man's costume is basically the same, also with the pleated front. He can wear armlets, bracelets, necklaces and earrings. His belt is made of silver mango leaves. Both dancers wear ankle bells.*

---

Essentially it is a dance for men, and about twenty-four ankle-length skirts are worn with a decorated red wool or cotton jacket, a long white scarf with white and red cotton lotus blooms on the end and a large head-dress shaped like a temple with a halo, studded with gold and jewels.

The Kathak style of the north consists of both men and women wearing full, gathered or pleated *ghagra* skirts with a *choli* for the women and a long-sleeved jacket for the man. Both sexes wear tight-fitting trousers, ankle bells and, often, the traditional forage or *topi* cap.

One of the most beautiful costumes comes from the east and is worn by the Manipuri dancers. Dark-orange or green skirts are stiffened from thigh to ankle and decorated with gold thread embroidery; tiny mirrors are also added. Over the skirt is worn a short, silver gauze, gathered skirt edged with a golden border. A coloured *choli* is worn with a fine gauze veil draped over a special hair style. Belts and jewellery complete this costume.

# TIBET

THE COUNTRY OF TIBET is divided into three main regions, Kham in the east, Amdo in the north-east and Utsang in the centre. In each region the costumes differ although the basic garment and style remain the same. There are two kinds of costume, those worn for special ceremonies and festivals and those for everyday use. Silk and fine cotton are used for special clothes, silk being imported from China and cotton from India. Wool is the only material that Tibetans produce and this is used for everyday clothing and for winter wear. Cotton is used in the summer months.

A material called *shema* is also made from the wool and this fine material is particularly durable and worn by the wealthier families. The finest wool is washed by hand and the coarser by the feet. The clothes of the lamas have always been woven by men. Various dyes are used for both the wool and the imported cotton: indigo from India and red from madder or obtained from an insect dye in Bhutan. Yellow is obtained from rhubarb and when blended with indigo produces various shades of green. Walnuts provide brown stain and 'off-black' is often used.

The basic garment is a long-sleeved coat called a *chubba* or *chupa*, which is folded across the body and held in place by an attached belt. Both men and women wear this garment and both have the draping from left to right, as is customary in Asia.

In the summer, Kampas women from the Kham wear only the left sleeve of the *chupa*, the empty right sleeve being tucked into the waist. This fashion shows the contrasting sleeve of the blouse. Amdo women also follow this style. Decorated boots in felt and leather show just below the skirt and in Kham the boots have very turned-up toes. In winter, warm sheepskin hats decorated with fur are worn but in the summer they will often go bare-headed.

The men's *chupa* always has sleeves and can be made from wool, cotton or patterned silk, according to the season of the year or the occasion. This *chupa* also has very long sleeves, which are folded back as required. The *chupa* is ankle length, but can be pulled up over a belt, giving a loose blouse effect. Young men tend to wear their *chupas* shorter, as do the men from Kham, who wear them knee length, and those from Amdo, who have them just below the knee. The *chupa* is worn during the summer months in the same style as that of the women, with the empty right sleeve tucked into the belt and showing a high-necked linen or cotton shirt with long sleeves. Loose, baggy trousers are tucked into decorated felt or leather boots. Large sheepskin hats are very popular as are those made from fox, wolf or mink fur.

# AFGHANISTAN

COTTON AND WOOL are the main materials used in Afghanistan and these are woven and dyed and made into garments by each family or group. In common with other Muslim countries, the women are veiled.

The very full *chadri*, which covers a woman from head to foot, with a latticed slit for the eyes, is still to be seen. The *chadri* is made of cotton in shades of blue, brown or black. In the country the women working on the land dispense with this, but cover their faces or hide themselves in the presence of strangers.

The women near the Pakistan border wear long, full trousers, often red in colour, with a loose, long-sleeved tunic dress, rather like the *kameez*, together with a draped headscarf. This is the basis of many of the women's costumes and the tunic varies in length and design.

In the northern areas striped material is used, often dyed red from madder or in shades of blue and brown. Loose, sleeveless, hip-length jackets are worn or a full-length striped coat for warmth.

Young girls go bareheaded, but women cover their heads with long headscarves, the colours of which vary according to the groups to which the women belong. The scarves are tied around the head, leaving a long end hanging down the back, which can be drawn across the face. A white headscarf signifies the married status.

Children are often barefooted, but adults wear sandals or a form of boot as protection against the rough mountainous ground or earth. The hide comes from the shaggy yak, which is found throughout the highlands of central Asia.

At puberty the girls of the nomadic Kushi group are given a dress which they must never take off, not even to wash it. As they grow, bands of material are added to the hem. If marriage or some other circumstances provides a new dress, it is worn over the old one, giving a bulky appearance.

Another form of dress is the long-sleeved, ankle-length *chupan*. This is a long coat made in wool, often white in colour and worn by the mountain people in the winter months. The *chupan* is worn over loosely fitting jackets and trousers, or is wrapped around the body like a cloak. There is also a similar type of coat that is made in stripes of darkish colours.

In the winter thick woollen, hand-knitted stockings are worn with leather boots. In the cities, the open-toe sandal is very common and sometimes shoes with up-pointed toes are seen. There are various forms of head-gear, which include the large turbans with a long end hanging down the back, neat round astrakhan hats, woollen knitted hats and large fur sheepskin hats.

*TIBET AND AFGHANISTAN. The woman comes from Utsang, a province in the centre of Tibet, and the man is wearing a typical worker's costume from Afghanistan. The woman is wearing the basic garment, a* chupa. *The length of this coat, with or without sleeves, and the material differ according to the region, the seasons and the occasion. The coat worn by the women of Utsang is sleeveless, which allows the coloured blouse to be shown. Underneath the* chupa, *the woman wears two blouses, one with very long sleeves and the other with slightly shorter sleeves. The long sleeves are folded back for work, but for dancing and other festive occasions they hang loosely. A feature of the costume is the apron. This is made in panels of light stripes. Decorated boots in felt and leather show just below the skirt. The man has a thigh-length, long-sleeved shirt that is belted at the waist, giving a skirt effect to the lower half. A sleeveless waistcoat is worn over the shirt, and his trousers are loose-fitting. In colder weather a jacket is worn, or the* poustine, *a coat made from sheepskin.*

# CHINA

THE FAR-FLUNG COMMUNITIES of the People's Republic of China each maintain their own cultural traditions. In the east and in the large cities and towns both men and women wear the blue or grey, long-sleeved, cotton denim jacket and trousers which are padded with cotton in winter, giving the jackets a quilted look. Children wear coloured jackets, often in bright red. Peaked caps are very popular. Simple lightweight shoes are worn.

In the five southern provinces the Maio, Tung and Yao people wear different costumes, although all are based on trousers and jackets. Women favour black trousers; Tung women have a band of white together with green and white braid around the edge of the trousers. A hip-length, pale-green jacket is worn tied around the waist with a black sash which has embroidered ends and a long white fringe. Jacket sleeves are also decorated with white braid. A white turban is tied around the head. White socks and red sandals are popular.

Maio women wear calf-length trousers over which is a short black skirt, a maroon or coloured jacket and a striped apron. These women are also distinguished by the wearing of tight gaiters reaching from the knees to the ankles.

Yao women wear hip-length, black jackets or tunics split at the sides; a coloured sash is tied around the waist. Red, white and blue braid decorates the hem and the split seams. They wear pointed black hats and down the front of the jackets silver plaques are fastened. When working in the rice fields, they are barefooted and the trousers are gathered into a band at the ankles. Cotton is mainly used and the embroidery and braiding is made in a cross-stitch pattern. There are numerous costume variations.

Men follow a similar pattern of dress with a tunic jacket and loose trousers. Jackets vary in length and are tied around the waist with a coloured sash making the costume both serviceable and economical. Large straw hats are worn both by men and women and the men wear either light shoes or go barefooted.

In the Sinkiang Vighur Autonomous Region in the far west, many different nationalities are found: the largest groups are the Moslem Vighurs and Kazakhs. The former group are mainly agricultural while the latter are pastoral and more equestrian. Vighur women wear the loose-style, long-sleeved tunic dress in shades of dark red or in patterns of purple and white. Over the dress is a black or dark-coloured sleeveless waistcoat. Brightly coloured embroidered skullcaps are worn. The long hair is plaited; the married women have two plaits and the younger girls have a number of plaits, according to age.

Men wear long tunic coats in stripes or plain colours and the older men favour

CHINA. *These two young dancers are wearing the typical jackets and trousers on which so many Chinese costumes are based. The method of fastening the jacket on the right side can be seen in numerous folk costumes throughout China. This feature can be traced back through many dynasties.*

*The dancer on the left has a jacket worn by the Han ethnic group, the largest in China. This type of jacket is worn for folk-dance presentations such as dances with fans, drums, long scarves, ribbons or those with a work theme. The colours range from pastel shades with contrasting borders to stronger colours such as turquoise. The trousers can be in the same material or in a different colour. The jacket worn by the dancer on the right is also from the Han ethnic group. The colours range from pastel shades to stronger colours with contrasting borders. A belt can be worn with both costumes and sometimes a little plain or decorated apron. The double panel is fastened at the back. Dancers using fans, lanterns and swords usually dress in this style. This style of jacket is fastened down the front with small braided buttons.*

CHINA. *This couple are
from different parts of China. The
woman is a horse-rider from the Inner
Mongolian Autonomous Region, which is in
the north of China. The man is a Yis from the
south-west. The people in Inner Mongolia live a
vigorous and often nomadic life. The woman
wears a thick coat (a del) which is simple and
adaptable; it is designed for riding and to
sustain some of the harsh weather conditions.
Under the coat she wears full baggy trousers,
tucked into firm, warm boots. This costume is
typical for both men and women. A bright green*

*sash is tied around the waist. Hats can vary
from turbans, as shown here, to round felt hats
decorated with coloured beads, woollen hats or,
for the men, sheepskin, astrakhan or felt hats
with brims. The man wears a long, loose jacket
which is worn over a full skirt together with a
cloak. The jacket can be white, pale blue or
black with contrasting braiding and decoration.
His unusual turban can be black or red. At one
time he would go barefooted but a modern touch
is introduced by the lace-up canvas shoes.*

darker shades. A triangular folded scarf is tied around the waist. Long trousers are worn with slippers, or are tucked into boots.

Kazakh women are distinguished by their long colourful dresses, which have three or four rows of frills at the hem. Over the dress is a knee-length, fitted, long-sleeved coat. Married women wear black or dark colours and the young ones are in stripes of green, orange and white. Their shoes have slightly turned-up toes.

Married women wear a long white head-scarf which is folded across the front of the head and leaves the ends hanging down the back.

Younger women wear embroidered, round, velvet hats which have a feather in the back and the hair is in a long plait. Light, low-heeled shoes are very popular.

The men are also very colourful in long, loose trousers, short, hip-length, decorated jackets and dark coloured turbans. They wear lightweight shoes.

# THAILAND

SILK HAS BEEN SPUN and woven in Thailand for nearly 2,000 years and the country is famous for its Thai silk in peacock colours of turquoise, gold, scarlet and flame. Working clothes are made in cotton and silk is used for special or festive occasions. Thai women wear the wrap-around type of sarong skirt, or *prasin*, together with a neat-fitting, long-sleeved jacket. In the north a draped sash or *sabai* is worn over the left shoulder.

On the klongs of Bangkok is the floating market in which the women sell their fruit and vegetables from low-sided boats. They wear brightly coloured *prasin* and loose-fitting, hip-length jackets, blue being a particularly favourite colour. They wear specially shaped straw hats to protect themselves from the sun. On the land and in the rice fields, a black jacket and *prasin* is the usual garb, and the women tuck the material through their legs to form a kind of trouser.

The region around Chiangmi in the north is very different from Bangkok. It is the centre of folk art and they make silver jewellery, painted paper umbrellas and a fabric that is a mixture of Thai silk and cotton. The *prasin* here are distinguished by woven borders and coloured stripes, which are in contrast to the plain material worn in the south.

Costumes worn by the hill tribes consist of black jackets with plain or brightly striped sleeves, black skirts, black trousers, long coloured panels, rather like aprons, wide sashes and short skirts, worn with gaiters reaching from ankle to knee. There is also a bright red costume.

Each tribe has a distinctive head-dress: close-fitting hats, which are decorated with silver coins, beads, woollen pompoms and fringes. Sometimes the hats are kept in place by means of chains under the chin. Around the neck hang large silver rings, necklaces and chains with silver discs attached. Silver linked belts are worn over sashes and jackets.

The men follow a similar pattern of dress to the women, with a loose shirt or jacket worn over the sarong-type of skirt. When working in the fields, black calf-length trousers are worn with a black shirt and a black and white scarf tied around the head, or a straw hat. For folk dancing the tunic shirt and trousers are in shades of blue, red or gold, with a sash tied around the waist. In the hills of the north, black predominates and there is a variety of costumes based on long black trousers, black jackets and coloured sashes.

The costumes worn by the dancers of the Royal Thai Classical Dance Company are illustrated on page 173. Masks are often worn to show the characters the dancers are performing in the ballet, or the dancers perform a masked play known as *Khon*. The stories are from the *Ramayana* or the *Khon Ramakien*, and the dancers portray the deities Rama, Sita, Laksmana and others, as well as demons and birds.

# KOREA

As with their near neighbours in the west, Koreans have bred silk-worms for centuries. As each family has to be self-supporting, the cotton, silk and hemp required for costumes is woven in the homes. Cotton is used for most clothes with hemp for hard-wearing garments and for the very poor; silk is only used for occasions such as weddings or special celebrations and then stored away.

Young girls, children and the Kisang (the professional entertainers), wear brightly coloured costumes, often in reds and yellows. The young women favour pastel shades of pink, blue and aquamarine and the older women wear mostly white, although it is a colour that can signify mourning. The period of mourning is for three years and so it becomes a predominant colour and is often worn continuously.

The use of colour is important in Korea and is associated with five points or directions. North is represented by the colour black; south is red; west is white; east is blue; and the centre is yellow.

Women's costume consists of a high-waisted skirt gathered into a yolk, the dress being called a *chima*. A petticoat, or *sokchima*, cut in the same style, is worn underneath, together with loosely cut trousers. A high-waisted over-blouse or jacket, the *chogori*, is tied on the right side with a bright ribbon. In Korea both the

men and the women fasten their garments from the left to right. White socks and small black slippers are worn.

For a wedding the *chima*, made of silk, is very colourful; for example, in red with an over-blouse of green that has bands of red and yellow on the sleeves. A beaded crown is worn from which hang long coloured ribbons that fall down the back and are decorated with jewels. Mothers carry their babies on their backs by wrapping round themselves a bright red, pink, green or black quilt into which the baby is placed.

Men wear white baggy trousers called *paji*, which end in cuffs fastened at the ankles. A white shirt with loose sleeves is worn under a sleeveless white or black waistcoat which buttons up the front. A pocket hangs from the trousers' waist-band. For very formal occasions a long white coat, the *torumagi*, is worn. Straw hats are usual and there is an old-style black horsehair hat shaped like a Welsh woman's head-dress.

Farmers celebrate festive occasions with folk dances and songs and decorate their costumes with bands of coloured material. Over their white waistcoats, in a cross pattern, they tie bright green, yellow, red or pink bands with a coloured sash around the waist. A band of red material is tied around the forehead and knotted in a bow over the left eye. They also wear an unusual hat with a round, turned-up brim

THAILAND AND KOREA. *Both the dancers are from the Royal Thai Classical Dance Company. The little girl watching is from Korea. The Thai girl wears a tight-fitting bodice, rather like a leotard, which can have sleeves or be sleeveless. Her skirt, the* sampot *or* panung, *is made of silk, silver or gold brocade and is 2.7m (9ft) long and 1m (3¼ ft) wide. The* sampot *is pleated in front to allow for movement and held in place with a belt that has a jewelled clasp. The broad cape, which is lined, reaches to calf length at the back. The front section passes over the shoulders, curves down to the waist and fixes into the belt. The material is heavily decorated with metal thread. A broad, jewelled collar, armlets, necklaces and bracelets are all extra accessories. To*

*complete the costume is the temple-style head-dress, the* tchedah *or* mkot. *This is very heavy as it is made of metal and encrusted with jewels. Before a performance the dancers are sewn into their costumes. The boy wears an even more elaborate costume with a tight-fitting, silver-thread brocade jacket that has epaulettes and a richly embroidered collar. He also wears a* sampot *but the material is taken between the legs and fastened at the back, forming a type of divided skirt. From a belt hang three embroidered panels. His gilt and jewelled head-dress is slightly different in shape from that of his partner. The little girl wears a pink dress called a* chima *and underneath is a white petticoat, a* sokchima, *cut in the same style. She has loosely cut trousers and a little jacket tied on the right side with a bright ribbon. White socks are worn with black, soft slippers.*

which is held on the head with a band under the chin. On the crown of the hat there is a tuft of crane's feathers fixed to a swivel button; the wearer can swing the feathers with a movement of the head.

The feathers are sometimes replaced with long paper streamers. In one famous dance the central performer rotates his head and swings the long ribbon in circles around his body – not an easy feat.

# JAPAN

THERE ARE FOUR TYPES OF DRESS to be found in Japan: those for everyday use, those for special or festive occasions, the work clothes for those on the land and the very elaborate costumes worn for the Noh and Kabuki plays. Materials used are linen, cotton and silk. Linen is the oldest material known to Japan; at one time flax was grown and woven by almost every family. There have been great changes since the production of modern materials, patterns and colours. Young people tend to wear bright colours and the older generation favour darker tones. The traditional patterns represent the characteristic features of both the country and the seasons.

For everyday wear both men and women wear the kimono. This garment dates back to the twelfth century and remains a practical and elegant dress for modern times. Although not suitable for city wear, for which Western styles are favoured, within the home a simple kimono is usually worn. The very informal kimono has shorter sleeves than the more conventional garment. In the summer the kimono is made of a light cotton and is known as a *yukata* and is worn over an undergarment. In the spring and autumn the kimono is lined and in the winter it is padded and worn over a cotton *yukata*. A short coat known as a *haori*, which is sometimes lined, is also worn over the kimono in winter, for formal occasions or when out of doors.

The long-sleeved kimono, or *furisode*, was originally for children, but is now also worn by unmarried women. Married women's sleeves are shortened and children's kimonos are made with tucks along the shoulders and around the waist, which are let out as the child grows. The kimono is always folded in a special way before being placed in a drawer. Silk kimonos are always very carefully cleaned; the garment is unpicked and each piece cleaned separately before being resewn.

Cotton is the most popular material for everyday use but is replaced for special occasions by silk. No buttons are used in the fastening of the kimono and it is

JAPAN. *This couple are dressed for an important occasion and so are wearing very formal kimonos. The woman is wearing a kimono called a* chuburisode *which, according to the colour and pattern, can be worn at weddings, a New Year's Eve tea ceremony or a party. The sash, or* obi, *can be tied in many different ways, the* length and width varying according to the material. The woman has chosen the* nagoya obi, *which is tied at the back in a special bow. She also wears white socks and leather-thonged* zori *sandals. The man wears a very New Year's kimono, known as a* haori. *The kimono is made of dark-blue silk, over which he wears a pleated skirt, the* hakama. *This is made in a pattern of fine stripes. A loose coat with his family crest embroidered in white is worn over the kimono and* hakama. *The coat is called a* haori *and is popular with both sexes. He wears a belt around the hips and has a silken cord around his neck with the two tassels tied in a special way. His socks and shoes are similar to the woman's.*

draped across the body from left to right and held in place by a deep sash known as an *obi*.

At her wedding a bride wears a very elaborate kimono; over a white or pastel-coloured kimono, either patterned or embroidered, is worn a long-sleeved *furisode* in the same material. Sometimes there is a second coat over the *furisode*. The bride's hair is specially dressed and a white or pastel hat, decorated at the back with flowers and with flat sides, is fixed on to the complicated hair style. These elaborate hair styles are now only seen on special occasions or are worn by the geishas. White socks with a split toe, called *tabi*, are worn with all kimonos, both by men and women.

The most popular form of footwear is the wooden *geta* or the *zori*. The *geta* was originally designed to keep the feet clean in the muddy streets. The flat wooden sole is supported by two lateral slats and the shoe is kept on by two thongs, which pass between the first and second toes and divide over the top of the foot.

The *zori* have flat soles of woven straw, rush, flax and bamboo, covered with a material or leather. A similar thonging to the *geta* keeps the shoe on the foot. They are now worn by both men and women as formal footwear to match ceremonial kimonos.

The informal kimono for a man is made of cotton and is usually black, brown, grey or dark blue. Fine checks, polka dots or bird's-eye design are also

*Wooden* geta.

used. A belt is worn low on the hips and the sleeves are shorter than those for the women.

The basic work garment for women consists of a long-sleeved blouse or coat, loose trousers or *mompe*, a wide straw hat worn over a coloured or white headscarf and either bare feet, plaited straw sandals (*waraji*) the wooden *geta* or the *jak tabi*, a sock which has a durable rubber sole. There are many variations, according to region.

The coat can reach to the hips or be longer and split at the sides. Sometimes a kimono is worn and the skirt tucked into the *obi*, showing the working trousers or a white underskirt over the trousers, rather like an apron. Cuffs are often worn as a protection to the sleeves. Blue and white checked squares or patterned cotton material is very popular with white, blue or striped trousers. The head is covered by either the wide hat made from sedge, bark, bamboo and reeds, or a white or coloured headscarf.

For work, men wear the short, dark-blue cotton *hopi* coat or a loose shirt over trousers and they also wear the same wide-brimmed hat and footwear as the women. In the wet season special rainproof capes, made from straw, are worn.

Some of the most elaborate costumes are to be seen in the Kabuki and Noh theatres. All the roles are played by men and the costumes, which have not changed for hundreds of years, are handed down through each actor's family.

# THE PHILIPPINES

THE MUSIC, DANCES AND COSTUMES found throughout the islands of the Philippines reflect their many ethnic influences. The most popular costumes worn by the women are the *balintawak* style and the *patadiong*. The *balintawak* consists of an ankle-length, full-skirted dress in white or a pale coloured cotton. The bodice has a round 'boat neck' and short, wide, puffed sleeves. Over the dress is worn a second, but shorter, skirt in a contrasting colour which can be in large checks, a floral pattern or in stripes. The over-skirt is draped around the waist, in a V-line, with the point reaching nearly to the hem of the dress. The loose end falls over the left shoulder.

No shoes are worn with either costume except in the rainy season when wooden shoes, called *bakya*, are used. The women go bareheaded, except when working on the land or in the rice fields where a large-brimmed hat of woven bamboo and palm leaves, called a *salakot*, is worn.

In the mountain regions of the large northern island of Luzon, the Ilocano and Ifugao women wear short, tight-fitting, hand-woven skirts in colourful horizontal stripes, and outside these are white short-sleeved blouses and striped loose jackets. A coloured band is tied around the head, and they go barefooted.

One of the most attractive costumes is the 'Maria Clara'; based on the old style of dress, it shows European influence. Made in silk, fine cotton or taffeta, the full floor-length skirt will often have a train. White or pastel shades of blues, pinks and mauve are used or a broad stripe in a dark contrasting colour, black on white or deep maroon on pale pink. The skirt is worn with a blouse of the same pale shade, the wide loose sleeves reach to the wrists, and around the shoulders and the 'boat neck' a silk fichu or shawl is draped and caught at the waist. There are several versions of this style, some with very elaborate flower embroidery decorated with beads and pearls. The dress is often referred to as a *serpentina*, *siete cuchillos* or *paloma*. With this costume low-heeled shoes are worn.

In the Muslim south the costume reflects the Malayan background of the people. A gathered wrap-over or sarong type of ankle-length skirt is worn with a long-sleeved jacket fastening up the front to a V-neck. Jacket and skirt are in contrasting colours of blues, pinks and greens, and the women go barefooted.

The men's costumes are known as *barong tagalog* and consist of long cotton trousers and white, long-sleeved shirts worn outside the trousers.

When the women wear the *balintawak* style, the trousers are red or black with a white shirt. With the *patadiong* style, trousers and shirt are both white. To accompany the Maria Clara costume, the trousers are black and the white shirt or *camisa de chino* is extra long. Black shoes

THE PHILIPPINES. *The woman is dressed in the* patadiong *style of costume and the man in what is known as* barong tagalog. *The* patadiong *costume is very popular and consists of a sarong-type skirt worn with a blouse. The skirt has a large fold or pleat in front that allows the wearer to move freely. Large, bright check material is very popular and with this is worn a simple white blouse. The man's* barong tagalog *consists of a white, long-sleeved shirt worn over long cotton trousers. The trousers can be black, which are a little more formal or a colour, such as red. When working the trousers are rolled up to the calves.*

are worn with this formal costume, but the men are usually barefooted.

Wooden *bakya* in various shapes and sizes are worn in wet weather, but only in the villages and poorer areas. The men will sometimes wear a straw *buli* or *balangot* hat similar to a flat-topped Spanish *Cordobés* hat.

The mountain tribesmen wear only a loincloth woven in horizontal stripes. The Ilongots have a plain dark-blue or black cloth, with a coloured band wound around the hips. A long red or black band is tied around the head and no shoes are worn.

The men in the south of the Philippines wear an ankle-length sarong or skirt, in checked cotton with a loose, coloured shirt or jacket. A scarf is tied around the head and then knotted at the side, and they go barefooted.

# MALAYSIA

MALAYSIA IS SITUATED in the heart of South East Asia. In the north are Thailand, Myanmar, Laos, Kampuchea and Vietnam. To the south are Singapore and Indonesia and, to the east, the Philippines.

The main population lives in West Malaysia, the narrow strip of land known as Peninsular Malaysia. East Malaysia consists of Sarawak and Sabah, the large country that borders onto Indonesia. Malaysia is a multi-cultural nation of friendly people and different nationalities: Malays, Chinese, Indians and the indigenous people of Sabah and Sarawak. There are many lovely and interesting costumes to be seen. The Chinese and Indian communities, especially in their dances and music, follow the traditions of their countries and wear the costumes as illustrated on pages 160 and 168.

The basic Malaysian costume is a sarong for both men and women, a type of costume that is found in many parts of South East Asia. There are many variations on the sarong in colours, material and length. For working out of doors on the land women wear a short sarong reaching to just below the knee, together with a simple loose jacket. In many of the folk-dance presentations the dancers wear costumes based on those worn in palace ceremonies and by the court dancers. These are very beautiful, with the sarongs made in rich silk materials in blues and turquoise colours. The tops are tight, sleeveless and reach to the hips, and the bare shoulders and arms allow freedom for the lovely arm movements found in the court styles. With this type of costume very elaborate head-dresses are worn.

Another type of costume is worn that has a long, loose-sleeved tunic which reaches to the calves, under which is the sarong. A beautiful decorated yoke in a contrasting colour gives a touch of elegance. The costume can be pink with a black, decorated yoke or blue with a yellow yoke. On their heads they wear a curved type of head-dress that represents the curved-style roof of many of the local houses.

In Sarawak the sarongs are heavier in design and darker in colour, and they are worn with a long jacket. In Sabah, for the more tribal dances, tight, long black skirts are worn rather than a sarong, and are accompanied by elaborate jackets and head-dresses. There are many styles and variations in these two regions.

For working on the land or fishing, the men wear loose trousers and coloured shirts, and not always the short sarong. Straw hats shaped like a cone and worn over a type of head-band that is knotted at the side helps to protect the head from the sun. Women also wear a similar band around the head. For warrior dances such as *gayung ota-ota* the men wear tight, knee-length trousers and tight-fitting shirts with either a short sarong or a wide sash. The costumes for the different native tribes of Sarawak and Sabah – such as those worn when the men dance *ngajat* – are very elaborate. They include feathers and the men carry swords and shields.

*MALAYSIA. The couple are both wearing very popular costumes for an important occasion. The woman's sarong and jacket are made of silk. The gold filigree belt, necklace, earrings and hair ornaments are only worn for a special event or ceremony. For everyday or for work, the sleeves would be shorter and the jacket would not be so long or so elaborate. Belts would not be used and the material would be cotton. The sarong can be in a plain colour or in a check pattern for ordinary use, and in beautiful silk and brocade designs for more formal wear. The man accompanying the woman wears a shirt and trousers to match, with a short sarong around the waist. On his head he wears the popular songkok hat. The colour of the shirt and trousers can be in various shades: blue, turquoise, white or yellow. For a less important occasion the sarong would be made of cotton, either plain or in a simple pattern. Bare feet are used for dancing; otherwise a light sandal or shoe is worn.*

# INDONESIA

THERE ARE SEVEN MAJOR areas in the archipelago of Indonesia: Sumatra, which is the largest of the islands; Java, which accounts for more than half of the population; the Nusa Tenggara group (which includes Bali), Kalimantan, Sulawesi (the third largest island), Maluku and Irian Barat.

The most popular form of costume for both men and women is the long wrap-around skirt called a *kain* which varies in colour, design and material according to the region. It can be worn gathered or pleated in front, or wrapped across. Cotton is generally used, as this is grown and woven on the islands.

Indonesia is renowned for its famous batik designs, especially in Java where the material is patterned and then dyed by an intricate process which uses layers of wax. Some designs and colours were at one time reserved only for court circles.

For special occasions the *kain* is woven with metal thread, an expensive process as the metal has to be imported. The very elaborate *kains* used for weddings are passed down as heirlooms.

Over the *kain* the women wear a long-sleeved jacket called a *kebaya*. In Sumatra this resembles a long loose tunic that reaches to the knees and is worn with a length of material folded and draped over the right shoulder, known as the *sabai*.

On Timor, the *kebaya* is hip length, sleeveless and worn with a belt. The *sabai* is draped round the shoulders and tucked under the belt. In Bali a broad, coloured sash is worn around the waist over a short *kebaya*. When working in the rice fields the women wear very large, umbrella-shaped bamboo hats, known as *chapil*. In towns the women are usually bare-headed or have a simple head-covering of draped cotton or muslin. The Minangkabau women of western Sumatra wear head-dresses of folded material which form two points.

The men's costume is fairly simple and consists of a *kain* worn with a white shirt or a loose jacket, in a variety of colours, which is worn over the skirt. Baggy trousers are also worn, especially in Sumatra.

Head-gear varies and can denote rank as well as region. A chieftain of a village will tie a cotton turban in a special way: on Bali the turban is knotted in front; in Java certain officials knot it at the back. Straw hats of different shapes and sizes vary within the islands, the popular round black hat or *pitji* is universal. Mostly the men are barefooted apart from those who wear ·Western-style dress.

# MYANMAR

THE MOST POPULAR COSTUME for both men and women in the Union of Myanmar (formerly Burma) is the long wrap-around skirt or *longyi*. This is worn folded across the front and can be gathered in, the men tying it in a knot and the women tucking in the ends. A shirt or blouse is worn with the *longyi* or a type of shirt-jacket called an *eingyi* which is worn outside. Cotton is chiefly used although silk is also worn, or a mixture of both cotton and silk.

When working outdoors both men and women wear large, flat, straw hats. The men also tie a coloured handkerchief, often in the same materials as the *longyi*, around their heads.

In the Shan territory men are distinguished by broad cotton turbans in white or in coloured stripes and squares. The women have a folded white headscarf or turban. The most popular form of footwear is the flat, open sandal held on the feet by two straps.

In the Kachin region, very attractive costumes are worn by the women, consisting of black skirts edged with a red panel tied around the waist with a blue sash. Black, long-sleeved jackets are worn over white or black blouses and numerous strings of small red, blue and yellow beads cover the chest.

Tall, black hats are worn and large circular silver earrings. A type of gaiter reaching from knee to ankle is a feature of many of the Kachin costumes. In the same region, bright red skirts woven with a yellow border and pattern are fastened round the hips with belts of cane. Over a black jacket is a huge collar, made of silver discs, which covers the shoulders, chest and the upper part of the back. Silver ornaments, like a fringe, hang from the edge of the collar. Red gaiters match the skirt and the usual open sandals are worn.

The Lashi women, also from Kachin, wear similar costumes, but in blue and white with blue turbans and red bead necklaces. The women from the tribe known as Black Lisu wear a tight-fitting cap made from strings of red beads and white buttons and with tiny brass bells across the forehead.

Very unusual costumes are worn by the Padaung women who live in the hills of the Kayah region; these are one of the eight main ethnic tribes and Padaung means 'long neck'. The women are often described as giraffe-necked as they have numerous brass rings around their necks. A long neck is much admired and at a special ceremony and feast, called a Waso, held when the moon is full, little girls of five have their first brass ring

*Gaiter worn by women in Myanmar, south-west China and Thailand.*

put round their necks. As times goes on, more and more are added until the total can reach twenty-one. Brass rings are also placed round their legs, extending from the ankles to above the knees.

The costume worn is very simple, with a short, dark-blue skirt edged with red, a loose white tunic also trimmed with red and a short blue jacket. For working there is a plain cotton, short-sleeved smock. A headscarf is draped around the head, forming a type of turban.

Other tribes in the same region wear more colourful costumes, but above the calf and around each knee steel wire is coiled or, alternatively, loops of cane or lacquered cords. There is similar coiling on the arms from wrist to elbow.

The regional costumes of the men show very little change from the basic *longyi* and jacket. Often on the left hip they carry a large, coloured cotton or canvas bag as the costume has no pockets. In the remote mountainous regions of the north-west the men of the Naga tribe wear elaborate head-dresses which are made from bear's fur, the feathers of birds and the tusks of the boar. They also use tufts of animal hair and wear necklaces of beads and tigers' teeth. For dancing there is a very elaborate *longyi* worn with a white *eingyi* jacket and a small white headscarf tied in a knot with a bow at the back. Sometimes calf-length trousers are worn and the *longyi* is draped at the waist. White stockings are worn with or without sandals.

---

*INDONESIA AND MYANMAR. The woman on the left is from Myanmar and the one on the right is an Legong dancer from the Indonesian island of Bali. The Myanman woman is wearing a special dance costume. The tight-fitting skirt, or* longyi, *reaches from the waist to the calf. Onto the hem of the skirt is added a deep section of fine white cotton or organdie, which flows into a train. The upper bodice is sleeveless, although it is often made with sleeves. A white cotton transparent jacket is worn over the bodice. Pastel colours are usual for this type of costume, pale blues and pinks being very popular. White socks are worn and sometimes sandals. The Legong dancer is wearing a long piece of material called a* kain. *The material is wrapped around the body and reaches from the chest to the ankles. A deep torso band is also wrapped around the body. The long apron and collar are all made of soft leather and painted in gold. She also has a hip ornament that hangs down the back, also made in leather. The head-dress is made in leather which has been cut into patterns and painted. White frangipani flowers decorate the leather crown and the flowers are attached to tiny springs that tremble as the dancer moves.*

# NEW ZEALAND

THE MAORIS SETTLED MAINLY on the north island of New Zealand and developed an unique culture and civilization. Using flax fibre, they devised what is known as 'finger-weaving' or *taniko*; two sticks were placed in the ground and the top of the garment or the border to be woven was suspended between them. The fibre yarns were dyed black, yellow or a reddish brown and were knotted together with unbleached fibres to form taniko patterns. The dyes were obtained from various trees; black was made by steeping the fibres in a solution made from bruised bark followed by immersion in mud for several days.

The patterns on the clothing were always geometrical and those carved on wood were circular or spiral; all the patterns had recognized names and meanings. A common design is a downward zigzag pattern that denotes the path of the sea. Many of the traditional designs have been replaced by modern patterns and the use of flax in *taniko* has been replaced by wool and cotton which are worked onto canvas.

Feather cloaks are much admired and considered one of the most beautiful of the Maori traditional garments. The finest cloaks are worn by the chiefs and nobles. These cloaks consist of white feathers from a wood pigeon's breast and green ones from its back. The bluish-black feathers from the parson bird and red ones from parrots are also used; all these feathers were tied into the flax-fibre base.

Maoris also tattooed their faces and this was considered by the women as a mark of manly beauty. The males would have the whole of the face covered in circular patterns, but the women had only the lips and the chin tattooed.

NEW ZEALAND. *These two Maoris are performing one of the very popular action songs. The woman is wearing a bodice, or* pari, *made in a* taniko *design. The* piupiu *skirt is made from the leaves of the native flax. These are partially scraped bare of the fleshy covering to expose the fibres and dyed to produce a geometrical pattern. They are then rolled into tight cylinders and fastened onto a broad waistband. Under her* piupiu *she wears a red skirt. A headband, called a* tipare, *is worn across the forehead and around the head. Around her neck she wears a pendant made of jade. The man wears a similar* piupiu *to his partner but his reaches to just above the knees whereas hers is just below the knees. He wears either shorts or swimming trunks underneath. Across his body is a band called a* tatua.

# CANADA

WHEREVER THE NATIVE peoples settled in Canada they adapted themselves to their environment and made full use of the natural resources available. The tribes on the Pacific coast made use of the cedar trees for building houses and the bark was used in the making of costumes. Spruce was woven into a material for the making of hats used in bad weather.

The people of the plains were buffalo hunters and the animal skins were used for both their tents and for clothing. In the east the bark of trees was used for wigwams and animal skins for clothing. In the north the Eskimos responded to the demands made by the climate and made protective clothing from the skins of caribou and seals. It was the French who first colonized the shores of the St Lawrence and, finding themselves ill-equipped to meet the climatic conditions, were greatly helped by the native tribes who taught them how to make moccasins, fur mittens and clothing from buckskin.

The early tribal costumes were mainly based on the wrap-around skirt, an apron or breechclout (a type of loincloth), leggings, cloaks and the poncho type of cape and shirts. The native peoples decorated their costumes with designs made from beads, woven braid, animal fur, quills and feathers. Each tribe had its own designs revealing identity and area. Patterns were inspired by environment and there were strong links with the natural world: trees, mountains and various animals were incorporated into geometric shapes. They held strong beliefs in supernatural power and thought that by the wearing of animal skins, feathers and claws, the strength and courage of the animal could be passed onto the wearer.

Beadwork was very popular and the tribes of the east coast used conch and clam shells to form beads. Inland, beads were made from stones, minerals and bones. The colours of the beads changed according to the area and tribe and, with the coming of the Europeans, designs began to change. By the late seventeenth century costumes became more ornate, with the use of embroidery and glass beads (obtained from the exchange of furs) and the use of appliqué work. Floral designs were used, especially by the Woodland tribes round the Great Lakes. It is thought that these designs were influenced by the embroidered vestments of the missionaries.

European traders also introduced silver coins, woollen blankets, mirrors, metal needles, thimbles and the use of iron tools. Waistcoats and shirts were worn by the men, and the women, who had previously worn skirts, now began to wear dresses with sleeves. By the nineteenth century many of the costumes had become very elaborate.

Although the Europeans influenced the form of dress of the native tribes, they had

# CANADA

CANADA. *The woman is an Eskimo and the man is Tlingit from British Columbia. The woman wears a costume that is based on the original standard design of tunic and trousers. This has changed very little over the centuries. The long-sleeved jacket, known as a parka, kooletah, amouti or atigi, is made from the skins of caribou. In the summer she would change the jacket for one made from a thick cloth or duffle material. The parka is embroidered with floral or with geometric patterns, depending upon the region. This woman favours a white parka, which is the most popular choice of colour. The* man is dressed for a ceremonial dance in a chilkat *blanket and wooden mask. The mask represents a raven, an important part of his tribal mythology. The blanket is made from mountain goat wool woven on shredded cedar bark. The design is first painted onto a pattern board by a man and then woven by a woman. Underneath the blanket he is wearing a decorated tunic, apron and leggings.*

little contact with the Inuit or Eskimo. Their form of dress has changed very little and is still based on the original standard design of tunic and trousers. In the summer months, when the daylight can last for 24 hours a day, the women wear cotton dresses under their parkas. The men and children wear lighter-weight trousers. On Sundays it was customary for the men to wear white duffle trousers replacing those made from polar bear skin.

Both men and women wear boots called *mukluks*, made from sealskin and into which the trousers are tucked. After being scraped, stretched and dried, the skin would become very hard and had to be chewed for several hours before it became soft enough for stitching! Different parts of the seal were used in the making of *mukluks* and caribou sinew for the stitching. The soles have to be replaced about every three months, depending upon the amount of wear. The hide from the seal's flipper is the most hardwearing. Women wear red or blue woollen stockings and thick mittens are worn by everyone.

Immigrants from most European countries have settled in Canada and the traditional customs of these ethnic groups has always been encouraged within the Canadian environment. The wearing of folk costumes and the performing of various songs and dances plays an important part in Canadian life today.

# USA

EARLY GROUPS OF MIGRANTS in North America soon adapted themselves to their local physical environments and developed specific cultures which formed the basis of the many ethnic tribes. In the USA there are roughly five different areas in which they settled, with an overlap into Canada and Mexico. They are: the eastern woodlands, the Great Plains, the southwest, the Plateau and Great Basin, and the North Pacific coast. Within these areas were seven major groups and numerous tribes.

The man's basic garment was the breechclout, a type of loin cloth made from deer or buffalo skin. Some tribes wore a short square apron, which covered the front and back. These were decorated with tribal designs. With the breechclout long leggings were worn, reaching to the tops of the thighs and made from soft leather and later from cloth.

A form of shirt called a 'war shirt' was worn by many tribes and was a garment used for ceremonial purposes rather than for war. Made from buckskin, the war shirt was decorated with braid, beadwork, tufts of horse-hair (and sometimes even with

USA. The woman is a Sioux and the man
belongs to one of the Woodland tribes of the
Great Lakes. The woman is recognizable as a
Sioux by the design across the yoke of the dress
and on her moccasins. The long fringed dress is
made of soft leather, either deerskin or elk.
Around her lower legs and ankles she wears
short leggings, which act as a protection against
injury from animals and snakebites. Her
moccasins are made from rawhide and
decorated with beadwork or quills. The
man is wearing a work costume, which
allows more freedom of movement, rather
than the elaborate ceremonial dress. He
wears an apron at the front and back
(which the Woodland tribe preferred,
rather than the more usual breechclout).
The design on the apron is made with
small beads, the front and back being
slightly different. The long leggings
used to be made of a soft leather,
but later on they were made from
the blanket cloth issued by the
American government. The leggings
were used for protection against the
weather and in hunting, as well as
for ceremonial purposes. He is wearing
a head-dress called 'The Roach'. This
is made from dyed horsehair and
shaped like a crest. The hair is fastened
onto a decorated head harness and
topped by a single feather. His
moccasins are very flexible; this suits
the forested countryside, and they are
ideal for hunting and canoeing.

human hair) or with animal skins or fur.

The Woodland tribe wore very distinctive shirts, black in colour with black leggings and aprons, all decorated with floral designs. Short capes and decorated yokes made from buckskin or the thick brown fur of the bear were worn by the north-east tribes. Waistcoats were probably copied from those worn by the European traders. Chokers, ties, cuffs and gauntlets are all modern additions. The fringed gauntlets were probably copied from those worn by the US cavalry.

A very striking part of the native North American costume is the magnificent feathered head-dress. First worn by the Plains tribes, it was later adopted by tribes in other areas. Made from eagles' feathers, it had great significance. The eagle is a bird much admired for its beauty and strength and a feather from this bird could be worn only after a very brave deed had been carried out. For very exceptional deeds more than one feather would be allotted, or a feather marked in a special way. The head of a tribe, or very brave warriors who earned a great many feathers, would wear a single or double row of feathers down the back.

There are numerous head-dresses amongst the various tribes, many being worn only on ceremonial occasions or for dances; often these head-dresses would represent buffaloes or eagles. The Iroquois and other eastern tribes wore round, tight-fitting caps of skin or feathers decorated with plumes.

They protected their feet with moccasins, a shoe adopted by the early settlers who found them more suitable for the terrain than the heavy European boot.

The moccasin can be made in two ways, either with a firm hard a sole of thick buffalo rawhide or with a soft leather sole.

The tribes of the south-west and the plains wore the hard-soled moccasins for protection against the stony ground and the cacti. Early native peoples and some tribes on the north-west coast and the southern plains went barefooted.

Each tribe made and decorated their moccasins in slightly different ways: if a scout found a discarded shoe he was able to tell which tribe it was that had passed that way. The Apache men wore a moccasin made like a boot with the upper part used as a protective covering around the calf. When this was not needed it could be turned down and used as a pocket in which to carry small objects. Short calf leggings were also worn by other tribes, but were separate and not joined to the moccasin.

The women's costume followed a similar pattern of style and development to that of the man. From a short, wrap-around skirt (which is still to be found among the ethnic peoples of South America) it gradually changed into a loose one- or two-piece dress. Climatic conditions as well as contact with Europeans did much to bring about the changes. Originally their costumes were made from the skins of deer, elk or other animals and changed very little among the tribes. From a simple dress there gradually developed more elaborate garments with beadwork, shells and appliqué as added decoration. The dress for work was fairly simple, but for ceremonial occasions much more elaborate.

With the coming of the Europeans and the life in reservations forced upon them, the women's dress changed and they wore

USA. This couple are dressed in costumes for a square dance. The many folk-dance groups that represent the USA wear the costumes based on the early settlers. This style of costume has now been considerably adapted from the originals. The women wear full-skirted, short-sleeved dresses in bright ginghams, as shown here, or spotted material with several white petticoats underneath. The dresses can have extra flounces on the skirt and added trim. The dancer is wearing low-heeled leather shoes; these can be either white or black. The man wears a check shirt in the same material as his partner, but this can be of a plain material and can have a decorated yoke with fringe or trim. Sleeves are usually long and either a knotted scarf or a knotted bow is tied at the neck. His trousers are dark, but these can vary in colour. Some men wear a cowboy-style costume with plain or striped trousers tucked into high boots.

full skirts and loose blouses made from cotton and calico and the use of skins for clothing ceased. Needles and thread were introduced and fibres made from animal sinews and the cactus thorn or bone needles were abandoned.

Necklaces have always been a feature of the tribal costume and these were made from shells, beads and braid woven with beads. In winter, blankets were wrapped around the body. The women's moccasins were made in the same pattern as those of the men.

With the discovery of North America, the colonists were attracted by the wealth of the New World. The majority of the immigrants were British, with a large Dutch settlement in the area which is now New York. The Spanish, attracted by the climate of California and Mexico, settled in those areas and the French stayed mainly in the Mississippi region. With this great

expansion of the population and the development of the land by pioneers, a new type of costume emerged for the cowboy.

The Great Plains, which were the home of millions of bison or buffalo, were occupied by the Plains tribes, whose way of life depended on the buffalo; they used the animals for food and buffalo skins for clothing and making tents. Soon, however, they were driven out by the pioneer immigrants and cattle ranches appeared. It was then that the familiar figure of the North American cowboy first emerged.

In common with the cowboys of Central and South America, the costume evolved to suit the occupation. This consisted of a type of leather over-trouser, or 'chaps', leather jackets or waistcoats, bright shirts, a gunbelt, heeled boots with spurs and large, felt 'Stetson' hats.

*A cowboy's riding boot.*

# MEXICO

THE INTRODUCTION OF European customs and also of Christianity into Mexico was never fully accepted by the indigenous peoples who blended their own strong culture with that of their Spanish conquerors. This is revealed in Mexican music, dance, design and costumes.

In the various regions there are numerous costumes to be seen and the variations are created by the purpose for which they are being worn – for example, work, fiestas, religious processions and dancing. The ancient cultures are seen in these costumes and in the more isolated areas women still spin and weave in the same way as before the Spanish conquest. Cotton thread or henequen fibre is spun on an old form of spindle and distaff. Lengths of material are woven on primitive looms consisting of a lengthways warp stretched between two sticks.

Many of the designs and embroidery used today are of stylized birds, animals, flowers and geometrical patterns, each region having its own traditional designs; the patterns have strong links with the old Aztec and Mayan beliefs. Colours also had a significance as the empire was divided into four regions with red for the east, yellow for the south, black for the west and white for the north.

The women's costume is based on variations of a *huipil* and *quechquemitl*. The *huipil* is a type of tunic dress or shift, worn mainly in the south, and it can be long or short, narrow or full in size and can be made from wool or cotton. In Oaxaca, a region that has numerous costumes, an ankle-length white *huipil* has wide horizontal bands of decoration around the skirt. From the same region there is a white *huipil*, which has flowers embroidered with brightly coloured silks down the front. There are *huipils* decorated with bands of pink and blue ribbons alternating with floral patterns or woven alternating stripes and geometric patterns. The *quechquemitl* is a type of triangular poncho that covers the upper body and is worn mostly in the northern and central regions.

From the central region of San Luis Potosí there is a white *quechquemitl* embroidered with bright patterns and from the east one with broad coloured bands decorating the border. The *quechquemitl* can be worn with the points either to the front and back or at the sides, and varies according to the region of origin.

The indigenous peoples adopted the skirt and blouse from European dress and adapted them to their own costumes. Skirts are usually full and of varying lengths and colours, under which there are several petticoats. In Vera Cruz, on the Gulf of Mexico, women wear long white cotton skirts ending in two or three layers of frills and with slight trains for fiestas. Above the skirt is a white blouse, a white

MEXICO. *The woman comes from Yucatan, which is the region on the peninsula that is the tip of the Gulf of Mexico. She is wearing a white* huipil *with flowers embroidered on the square neckline and around the hem. The* huipil *is a pre-Hispanic garment that has been retained by many communities, although it differs according to regions. In some areas the* huipil *tucks into the skirt or it may hang loose (as illustrated) or reach to the ground. The man is wearing one of the most colourful costumes found in Mexico. He is a Huichol from Santa Catarina in the west. The men's costumes are always made and embroidered by the women. The long tunic shirt, or* rahuarero, *and the wide trousers, or* shaveresh, *are both made from cotton. Several sashes are worn around the waist and the cape (*tuharra*) is of red wool. On a waistband or belt, called a* cosihuire, *are fastened small embroidered bags*

*decorated with red tufts. He is carrying two woven bags, one made in brown and white wool and the other in cotton, decorated in red as on the belt. The flat-crowned straw hat, or* reporero, *is decorated with balls of coloured yarn. From the brim hang butterfly cocoons. On his feet are leather sandals (*huaraches*).*

*quechquemitl* and a tiny black apron that is decorated with flowers.

A popular women's costume is the *china poblana*. The decorated blouse is of white linen and is embroidered with silk thread or glass beads. The skirt, or *zagalejo*, is in two tones with a contrasting section at the waist and hem. The skirts can be very elaborate and decorated with coloured sequins, sometimes forming the country's emblem. The national colours of red, green and white are popular colours for this dress.

The Tehuana women from the state of Oaxaca wear very full skirts made in a dark-coloured satin upon which are printed or embroidered large coloured flowers. These patterns are thought to have been inspired by the designs on the imported shawls from Spain. For the fiesta these skirts have a deep frill of white lace round the hem and are worn with a short matching *huipil* and an elaborate head-dress. Blouses are coloured or white, usually with short sleeves. Many of the white blouses have embroidery on the sleeves and neckline.

An essential part of the women's costume is the stole or *rebozo*. It developed from the need to cover the head in church as well as protection against the weather, apart from decoration. When slung from the shoulder it can be used for carrying a baby or the shopping. The *rebozo* are woven in bright colours and patterns or they can be quite plain. The Tarascan women

*Tehuana lace head-dress.*

of Michoacán wear a black wool *rebozo* woven with fine narrow blue and white stripes, which is worn with a black skirt, a bright sash and a square-necked embroidered blouse.

Not all costumes have head-dresses, the *rebozo* being a substitute covering, but the hair is often elaborately dressed. One of the most elaborate head-dresses is worn by the women of Tehuana; made of white lace it frames the face and the shoulders. The manner of wearing this head-dress denotes whether the occasion is religious or social. In Tlaxcaca, in the east, folded scarves are worn on the head or a half gourd, brightly painted, is tied on the head over a head-scarf.

The men's costumes are based on the European style of white shirts and trousers, but vary according to region. The shirt can be worn tucked into the trousers and with a bright sash tied at the waist, or it can be worn outside the trousers like a jacket. This jacket-style shirt, or *manta*, can be buttoned to the neck or worn with a knotted scarf. The Nahua from Puebla wear a loose-fitting, short-sleeved woollen tunic over their shirts. Known as a *coton*, this type of tunic is found in several regions, the Nahua wearing a deep purple one: in the Chiapas province they are in red and white stripes. The *coton* can be worn loose or belted.

In the Chiapas highlands, the men of the Tzotzil and Tzetzal tribes wear a type of tunic called a *chamarra*. This is a length of cotton material that has a

hole for the head and, when worn, the folds are carefully draped and tied around the body. White shorts are worn underneath or, if from Tenejapa, they are red. The men from Huistan wear a type of baggy loincloth instead of shorts. A feature of their costume are the sandals, which are made with ankle guards at the back, a style which goes back to the Mayas.

In the cold weather the men wear a woollen serape, not unlike a poncho but which opens down the front. When it is not in use it is folded and worn across the shoulders.

MEXICO. *The woman is wearing a popular dancer's costume that has a very full skirt and is based on those worn in Jalisco in the west. The dress is decorated with frills, lace and ribbons. The material is cotton and can be in any bright colour. Her hair can be in plaits or braids and is looped up and secured with many coloured ribbons. Sometimes the braids are woven with ribbons and taken across the head, as they are here. Brown or black shoes are traditional, although white shoes are also very popular. Usually she will carry a silk rebozo wrapped around the arms. The man is dressed in the costume most associated with Mexico. He is wearing a festive version of the* charro *or horseman's costume. In common with other cowboy costumes, the design is both functional and decorative. The short jacket allows freedom of movement and the tight trousers give protection when in the saddle. The shirt is of white cotton or linen and a long silk bow is tied at the neck. Silver buttons and cord decorate the trousers. The belt has a silver buckle and the edge of the large sombrero is decorated with silver thread. His riding boots have slightly raised heels which, like his partner's shoes, help to produce the heel beats found in the various Mexican dances.*

# GUATEMALA

WITH A STRONG INDIGENOUS majority, the way of life in Guatemala is very different from its neighbouring Central American countries. Living in the highlands and in the many villages around Lake Atitlán, the local people wear their costumes as part of everyday life and not just for fiestas or special occasions. They have a love of colour and pattern and each village has its own specially woven designs.

Cotton and wool are the main materials used and in Salcajá, a village in the Lake Atitlán region, material known as *jaspé* is woven. The yarn is first dyed and then the warps stretched by wrapping them around the modern telephone poles. Red is a very popular dye. Until the introduction of chemical dyes in the nineteenth century, Guatemala exported large amounts of cochineal and indigo, the source of reds, blues, purples and pinks which, together with green and orange, are the colours found in many of the costumes.

The women's costumes are based on long, ankle-length skirts which are woven or embroidered in stripes and various patterns. Green and purple wool is used in embroidery and the designs show stylized birds, people, stripes or rhythmic geometrical designs which come from the ancient Mayan culture. The skirts are narrow and sometimes have a gathered section. The old looms and manner of weaving produced material in a narrow width, which governed the cut of the costume.

A type of loose blouse called a *huipil*, which has various styles, colours and patterns, is worn. Sashes with woven designs are tied around the waist and a long scarf, or *rebozo*, is draped over one shoulder. Turbans are worn with most costumes and these range from a simple band to very elaborate styles; they are predominantly

---

*GUATEMALA AND HONDURAS. The boy and the woman on the right are from the region of Lake Atitlán in Guatemala. The woman is from the village of Santiago, which is situated by the side of the lake. Her costume is for work. The long skirt has been woven in colourful stripes and the loose blouse, called a* huipil, *is a garment found in many Central American countries. For working, the* rebozo *is draped over one shoulder. The little boy is from the Solola region. He is* wearing a bright, coloured shirt and striped trousers, with a skirt over the bright trousers. He is also carrying a black and white decorated canvas bag, an item which most men use to carry all their personal belongings. His hat is made of fine straw. Sandals or bare feet are usual. The little girl on the left comes from Honduras and is wearing a typical dress for school. It is only on fiestas or special days that the more elaborate costumes are worn.

red in colour. The women from Santiago, a village on Lake Atitlán, wear turbans that resemble halos. A long, narrow, red band about 11m (36ft) long has each end embroidered to the depth of 1m (3¼ ft) with geometrical patterns in orange, green and purple. The band is wound around the head with the hair specially arranged to give the required halo effect. At Zunil, a little village situated between two volcanoes, the women weave and wear large purple cloaks, the colour signifying the eventual eruption of the volcanoes and the destruction of the villages.

The men's costumes are equally colourful. The trousers are usually calf length, loose-fitting and made in a variety of colours ranging from plain white to striped patterns in shades of red, pink, blue, black and white. Multicoloured, long-sleeved, striped shirts are tucked into the trousers and a sash is also worn. In some villages the men wear jackets which are embroidered in bright coloured wools. Their sashes and trousers are also embroidered or woven with animal or quetzal bird designs, or in pink or purple stripes. For men floral designs are not used extensively.

The men from the village of San Antonio in the Lake Atitlán region, wear a black and white checked skirt, which reaches from the waist to mid-thigh, over their brightly striped trousers and shirt. In the village of San Juan the men wear loose tunic coats reaching to the knees and split up the sides, thus forming a type of apron. A red sash is tied around the waist and a red striped shirt is worn. The trousers are white. Many of the men carry a decorated canvas bag slung from the shoulder or tied around the waist. Hats range from the flat-brimmed Panama style to round crowned hats with narrow brims, these being decorated with coloured hatbands and ribbons. Both men and women either go barefooted or wear a type of sandal.

# HONDURAS

THE COSTUMES OF HONDURAS are based on the style which was popular in the mid-nineteenth century and have much in common with their neighbouring countries. Although European dress is worn mostly in the towns and cities, the local costumes are still popular in the villages, especially during fiesta times.

The women's dress changes according to region and occasion. For work it is very plain with simple coloured trimming and is made in calico or cotton. The Sunday and fiesta dresses are made of silk or cotton, embroidered with silk using old Mayan patterns and designs. For work a short white skirt has an added frill around the hem and is decorated with a band of coloured braid or coloured stitching. With this skirt is worn a white blouse with short puff sleeves, a round 'boat' neckline and a deep frill, a pattern which is very popular in so many Central American countries. The older women prefer a similar dress, but with a longer skirt and the blouse has a wider frill but no sleeves.

The more elaborate style of dress has a skirt with two layers of frills, a long-sleeved blouse with a high neckline and a deep frill around the shoulders. Another style of dress, worn either short or long, depending upon the occasion, has a blouse with elbow-length sleeves ending in frills and an inset front panel decorated with coloured braid: the skirt follows the usual pattern. Several strings of beads are worn, which have the local name of *lageimas de San Pedro*. The beads are made from dried seeds and thorns, which are painted in bright colours. The hair is usually worn in two plaits and the ends tied with bright ribbons. Open sandals are the usual form of footwear.

The men wear the typical costume of long white trousers, long-sleeved, white tunic shirts worn outside the trousers and red handkerchiefs that are tied around the neck. Straw hats are worn and their sandals are similar to those which are worn by the women.

# COSTA RICA

IN THE WOMEN'S COSTUMES of Costa Rica can be seen styles common to neighbouring countries. There are several variations, but all are based on the frilled blouse and full skirt. In the regions bordering on Nicaragua the skirts tend to be narrow, but those nearer to Panama have fuller skirts, not unlike the *pollera* (see page 205). For working the skirts are shorter, but longer styles are worn for galas, etc. The skirts vary in colour and range from white to a multicoloured effect.

The white blouses are made with round, boat-shaped necklines and have one, two or three frills embroidered in floral silk designs. For galas, the frills are more elaborately embroidered.

A coloured stole, or *rebozo*, is draped either around the shoulders or over the head. There is usually a cross, medallion or locket suspended from a black band around the neck and circular golden earrings recall the earlier native tradition. Lightweight shoes or sandals are mostly worn.

The most popular costume for the man consists of black or dark brown long trousers worn with a long-sleeved white shirt and a red knotted handkerchief at the neck. A coloured sash is tied around the waist and a long knife in a decorated leather sheath hangs from a silver chain worn over the sash. He wears a straw Panama hat and either sandals or Western-style shoes.

For work in the plantations, the long trousers are replaced by serviceable and comfortable shorts or there can be a form of skirt or kilt. With these are worn a white or coloured shirt outside the trousers.

COSTA RICA. *The women's costumes of Costa Rica have much in common with those found in other countries in this region. The full skirt has many variations and colours. This woman is wearing a full skirt in two colours and it is made with two deep frills. The white blouse has two layers of frills and has much in common with those found in Panama. She wears the coloured stole or* rebozo, *so very popular in Mexico. The man is wearing a typical costume consisting of black trousers, white, long-sleeved shirt and a red and yellow knotted handkerchief at the neck. Around his waist is tied a long coloured sash. Over the sash is a silver chain from which hangs a long knife in a decorated leather sheath which is used for work on the coffee plantations. He wears a straw Panama hat and Western-style shoes.*

# PANAMA

ONE OF THE MOST BEAUTIFUL costumes to be found in Central and South America is the women's *pollera* from Panama. This costume, which is made in cotton, has a very full, long skirt, a blouse top with short sleeves and a boat neckline draped with frills. The *pollera* is thought to be based on the seventeenth-century Spanish costume with its wide skirt of two or three flounces. This dress became adapted to the tropical climate of Panama. A simple version in white cotton was worn by women in the country and towns. The dress for the servants and slaves of prominent families became more elaborate and fine embroidery, chains, broaches and combs were added, showing the wealth of their mistresses. The great ladies themselves began to wear the *pollera* in public and the dress eventually became the national costume.

There are three styles of *pollera*, the one from the Los Santos province being the most elaborate. The costume from the provinces of Herrera and Veraquas are similar in style but without the embroidery and are made in pastel shades as well as white. The skirt has three tiers, unlike the Los Santos costume which has only two. Several chains are worn around the neck and also earrings. The hair is worn in two plaits and tied with ribbons and several gold-topped combs are placed in the sides and the back of the head. When the hair is dressed without the combs, a white, small-brimmed straw hat is worn.

A much simpler *pollera* is used for everyday wear, called the *montuna* or *diaria*. This has a full skirt made in two or three tiers and is in floral-patterned cotton. The white or pastel-coloured blouse is in the same design, but without an upper frill. The plaited hair is tied with ribbons and a white straw hat is worn.

With each costume a black velvet ribbon, with a cross, coin or medallion attached, is worn around the neck. For everyday wear an ordinary lightweight shoe or sandal is worn.

The men's costume consists of two styles, one to accompany the women's gala dress and one for everyday wear. The dress or formal *camisella* style has a white, long-sleeved, cotton shirt with a little stand-up collar. The front and back of the shirt is decorated with a row of fine tucks or open-work embroidery. The shirt is worn outside dark-blue or black trousers and the lightweight shoes are made of white canvas and leather. A shallow-brimmed straw hat is worn.

The *montuna* or country-style fiesta costume is similar in pattern, but the shirt and trousers are made in a heavy white cotton or linen. The long-sleeved shirt has a flat collar and a plain front, but the hem is fringed. The trousers reach only to the knees. For a fiesta the shirt is embroidered in petit point. The workers are barefooted or wear home-made leather sandals.

PANAMA. *The woman is wearing the* pollera de gala *costume, considered to be one of the most beautiful costumes to be found in Central and South America. This costume comes from the Los Santos province and is the most elaborate. It is made in fine white cotton and covered with exquisite embroidery, drawn-thread work and fine cross stitching. Valencian lace and the locally made Mundizzo lace are used on the frilled blouse. Underneath her skirt she has two wide, white petticoats. Several gold necklaces, a cross or locket on a velvet ribbon and a red pompom pin all add to the spectacular beauty of the dress. Her hair is parted down the middle and made into two buns either side. Two to five gold combs are placed in the back and sides of the hair and on either side she wears the* tembleques. *These are delicate ornaments made in the shapes of flowers, butterflies and leaves, which create a shimmering effect when she dances or walks. The man wears the country-style fiesta costume, known as* montuna. *His long shirt and knee-length trousers are made of a thick white cotton. There is embroidery on the cuffs on his long shirt sleeves, around the neck opening of the shirt, around the hem and on the trousers. His hat is made of the famous Panama straw.*

# CUBA

IN CUBA THE SPANISH INFLUENCE is dominant: the costumes have a similarity to those of other Latin American countries and a popular dress used in folk dance has the tight-fitting, hip-length bodice with a full skirt gathered into the hipline rather than the waist. The boat or scooped neckline has a wide frill, which covers the short sleeves.

A turban is tied around the head and often this is surmounted by a little straw hat. The dress is always in bright colours, made in cotton, and a white, spotted or pastel background is popular.

The men wear long trousers which can be rolled to the calf, and white is the usual colour. A loose shirt with long sleeves is worn outside the trousers and stripes or checks are popular as patterns.

Straw or felt hats with broad brims protect the head from the sun and lightweight shoes or sandals are worn by both men and women, although they are often barefooted when they are dancing.

# COLOMBIA

COLOMBIA IS A LAND of many contrasts and the costumes tend to reflect the differing climates and landscapes. The Andes mountain ranges split the country into various regions, which have all developed their own characteristics of music, dance and costume. In the mountain regions wool and dark colours are used, and the costumes show a strong ethnic influence. Towards the coastal areas a more European influence is shown. Colombia has two coastlines, one bordering on the Pacific and the other on the Caribbean. The music and dances show a strong rhythmic interpretation, especially from the Caribbean.

The women's skirts are ankle or calf length and made in cotton, either in black, brown, blue or more pastel tones, and are usually decorated with a profusion of flowers. Blouses are more colourful and are in white, coloured or flowered cotton. For special occasions, a white blouse with a boat-shaped neckline is decorated with two layers of white lace which forms a large round collar. These blouses have elbow-length sleeves ending in frills or cuffs.

In common with all Andean people, felt hats are worn by men, women and children, and the hats are in black or brown, shaped like trilbies and worn pulled down over the eyes. Straw hats can also be worn. Many of the women go barefooted, but *alpargatas*, or sandals, which are made from a coarse cotton canvas, are also worn.

The men also wear dark clothes with jackets and trousers of the same colour. Over these are worn a type of poncho or cape called a *ruana*; these are made in wool and range from oatmeal to black in colour, these colours being the natural shades of the wool. Sandals, if worn, are made of canvas.

# VENEZUELA

WITH THE DISCOVERY OF OIL in 1917, Venezuela became the richest of all the South American countries. Thousands of European immigrants poured into the country to work on the expansion programme and consequently many of the old traditional ways and also costumes were lost. Today the playing of national music is encouraged, especially the rhythmical *joropos*. The costumes show a strong similarity to other South American countries.

The women wear short-sleeved blouses with a boat or scoop neckline decorated with a frill. A full knee-or calf-length skirt is gathered into a waistband. The hair is worn in two plaits and is tied or plaited with a coloured ribbon. Straw hats with turned-up brims or long scarves are worn on the head.

Cotton is used for the costumes and on special occasions the blouse and skirt are in white or pastel shades of blue, yellow or pink. An everyday costume has a coloured skirt in a spotted or floral pattern. Spotted patterns are very popular, reflecting Spanish influence. A white blouse is usual for everyday wear, together with white or red shoes with small heels.

The men wear a loose, long-sleeved white shirt, worn outside the trousers, which are also white. This is the formal costume, but for work the trousers are rolled up to the calves and a short-sleeved, round-necked shirt is worn. Broad horizontal stripes are much favoured, with the coloured stripes standing out from a white background. A coloured scarf is knotted at the neck and a straw hat which has a turned-up brim is worn. The men are either barefooted, have sandals or wear formal shoes.

COLOMBIA AND VENEZUELA. *The woman in the middle and the man on the left are both from Colombia. The man on the right is from Venezuela. The woman comes from the region of Bogotá and is wearing a dark skirt and a flowered cotton blouse. She is wearing a straw hat over a large dark head shawl, which acts as protection against the sun. The Colombian man comes from the famous area known as the Llanos, which is a vast plain and a cattle-producing region. The cattle are tended by tough cowboys known as* llaneros. *When not in the saddle he would be wearing white or black trousers and a white shirt, but still with a knotted scarf – and no whip, of course. The Venezuelan man is wearing a working costume very similar to those found in other South American countries. He has white cotton rolled-up trousers, a loose shirt with turned-up sleeves, the typical red scarf and a straw hat. He is wearing sandals but, according to the job, he might be barefoot.*

# BRAZIL

THE POPULATION OF BRAZIL embraces many different racial and ethnic groups. No definite costume has been established as people adapted their own national costumes to the climate and terrain of their new country.

One of the most colourful costumes worn is that of the Bahia women. Floral-patterned, long cotton skirts and white blouses are worn with brightly striped turbans, stoles and numerous long neck-laces of small coloured beads, all of which reflect their West African ancestry. Carnivals are very popular in Brazil, and many elaborate costumes are displayed, but these are mainly created for the occasion. The women's two-piece costume with the frilly sleeved top, short flounced skirt and exaggerated turban does show an ethnic background.

Two very large cattle-breeding areas are found in the north-east and the south. A cattle ranchhand's life is a hard one and their costumes have been evolved to suit their way of life, much of which is spent in the saddle.

In the north-east the *vaqueiros* or *boiadeiros* (cowboys) roam the vast plains. The gauchos who live in the south are very different in outlook, dress and physical appearance to the *vaqueiros*, as the climate in the south is less harsh. Black or grey loose trousers are tucked into black leather boots; a sleeveless waistcoat is worn over a long-sleeved shirt and a long coloured scarf is tied around the neck. A black or grey felt hat with a wide brim is worn.

There are various indigenous tribes whose way of life seems to have changed little over the centuries. They wear very little, but have a great sense of colour and create fantastic ceremonial head-dresses; these are made from natural materials, including feathers and leaves. They also paint their bodies in intricate patterns and designs.

# BRAZIL

BRAZIL. The woman wears a long dress, which is like those worn by the early European colonists. This type of dress and style can be found in numerous countries. Made in cotton, it has lace trim. The man is a vaqueiros, or cowboy, from the vast plains in the north-east. He is accustomed to a hard life and wears a costume made entirely of leather, apart from a cotton shirt. The leather garments become hard from wear and act as a protection from the dangerous and sharp needless of the cacti. His trousers are tucked into strong, brown riding boots.

# PERU

THE ART OF WEAVING, dyeing and the use of colours and patterns, all showing strong Inca influence, are still in use in Peru today; it is also reflected with European influence in the costumes. In Peru there is a very large indigenous population who live mainly on the plateau and the mountainous regions. These communities are almost self-supporting, weaving their clothes from the alpaca, llama and sheep wool. The old form of belt or vertical weaving is still in use, a form used by the Incas. The two main groups are the Quecha and the Aymará.

The women wear full, gathered, handwoven skirts, black being the popular colour. It is unusual to find dark shades in South America, but the use of black has been attributed to mourning for the last Inca ruler. Black skirts are worn in the region of Cuzco as well as other loyalist areas. A touch of colour is introduced in the bright border of the hem and the trimming on the jackets. In the mountain regions the women favour blue or green skirts. For weddings the black and coloured skirts are replaced by red ones.

Skirts are worn one on top of the other and are all in different colours, which are very effective in dancing the *huayno*. The numerous skirts also give added warmth during the highland winters. White or brightly coloured blue or green long-sleeved blouses are worn, either separately or under jackets. A short cape or *mantas* is worn either around the shoulders or over the head, fastening under the chin. Made in a woollen material, it reflects Spanish influence.

A flat hat with a slightly turned-up brim is worn either over the cape or *manta* or over the knitted helmet or *chullo*. Sometimes a felt hat is worn in black or light brown. One hat is often worn on top of another and they are seldom removed, except to sleep. If the hat has flowers in the band it means that the wearer requires a husband. Feet are bare or sandals are worn.

The men wear calf-length or long trousers, usually black and worn with a shirt, waistcoat or coat. Over a coloured sash a belt is sometimes fastened. A brightly coloured poncho or open serape is an essential part of the costume. The headgear is the same as the women's, but the knitted *chullo* is worn with both styles of hat, especially in the winter. Bare feet or simple sandals are usual. For their celebrations and religious processions, special costumes are worn, highlighting their love of colour, as well as festivities.

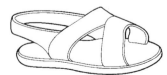

*South American sandal.*

PERU AND BOLIVIA. *The couple on the left come from Peru and the woman on the right is an Aymara from one of the many villages around Lake Titicaca in Bolivia. The Peruvian woman is wearing a heavy woollen skirt with many layers of coloured skirts underneath, usually up to about ten. When a dancer turns the many skirts are then revealed. The bright red jacket is decorated with buttons and braid. The flat hat is worn over a cape, but sometimes the cape is draped around the shoulders. The top of the hat is decorated in a pattern similar to the one that the man is holding. Bare feet or flat sandals are usual. The man wears the traditional brightly coloured poncho over a shirt, waistcoat or jacket. The warm, woollen, knitted* chullo *that he wears on his head is especially needed in winter. The woman from Bolivia wears a similar style of costume to that of her Peruvian neighbour. Her full skirt also has many layers of underskirts. The top skirt is usually of a bright colour such as red. The long-sleeved, loose blouse can be replaced by a little jacket or tucked into the skirt. The shawl that is tied in front may be of vivid colours or plain, as illustrated.*

# BOLIVIA

MORE THAN HALF THE POPULATION of Bolivia are indigenous and a third are mestizo, a mixture of indigenous and Spanish; the two main groups are the Aymará and Quecha. Life is primitive and the mode of living and dress has changed very little over the years: many indications of the Inca civilization are still evident. For clothing, cotton and wool are the main materials. The coarse, hard-wearing, woollen cloth is made from alpaca and llama wool.

Their love of colour is shown in the women's bright skirts, or *polleras*, under which numerous coloured petticoats are worn. The skirts are in red, pink, light blue, dark or light green. A vividly coloured, long-sleeved blouse is worn outside the skirt and around the shoulders is worn a woollen cape or shawl. These are orange, pink, red or checked in colour and are often fringed. Bolivian babies are carried on their mother's backs in a blanket which is knotted in front and worn over the shawl. A feature of the costume is the bowler or derby hat. Made in felt, the wool is first soaked, pounded and then starched or moulded. The favourite colours for these hats are brown, beige, black and grey, all of which are the natural colours of the wool. Occasionally white is worn, but white llama pelts are rare and valuable and, consequently, saleable. The bowler hats are always removed when the women enter church.

Another hat is made of white straw and is shaped like a top hat or similar to the hats of Welsh women. These are very popular in Cochabamba. Large ponchos are worn instead of capes.

Men wear dark trousers, which reach either to the calf or to the ankle. Around the waist is a sash or belt and in summer sleeveless waistcoats in bright colours are worn over a shirt, and always a felt or straw hat. In the colder regions and in winter, the vividly woven poncho is worn. The poncho is a piece of material with a hole for the head. Also popular is the serape, which is similar to the poncho, but has an opening in the front. In some regions white linen, calf-length trousers are worn with a short poncho in bright red, yellow and black stripes. A woven pocket or pouch with a fringed edge hangs from the waist.

A very popular form of head-gear is a knitted or woven, tight-fitting helmet called a *llucho* or *chullo*. This can be plain, patterned in a geometrical design or ornamented with round suns and stylized llamas. It can be extremely cold in the high Altiplano area and this type of cap, with its long earflaps, is essential for warmth. A felt hat is worn over this if necessary.

Both men and women go barefooted or wear a homemade leather open sandal. The Bolivians have a great love of carnivals at which the most colourful and elaborate costumes are worn.

# PARAGUAY

THE COLONIZATION OF PARAGUAY by the Spaniards was not extensive and the Paraguayans have retained many Guarani characteristics.

The women wear a dress that shows a strong Spanish background and which is similar in style to those found in other South American countries. Full cotton skirts made in bright colours are worn over white petticoats.

On Sundays or festive occasions very full skirts are more elaborate with one or two deep frills around the hem in contrasting colours. The Paraguayans have a love of colour and reds, blues, pinks and bright primary colours all create a vivid effect.

Blouses vary in style, with the round boat neck being very popular, and there are short puff sleeves, loose sleeves which reach to the elbows or long tight sleeves. The neckline is decorated with embroidery or a deep frill. Blouses can be in white cotton or of the same material and colour as the skirt, or in a contrasting shade.

Straw hats have round crowns and large flat brims and at fiesta time these hats are decorated with flowers or painted in bright floral patterns. Silver necklaces are very popular, both with old and young Paraguayans. Sandals or European heeled shoes are the usual form of footwear.

The men, when working on the cattle ranches, wear the typical cowboy dress of full, baggy trousers, either in black or brown, which are tucked into boots of a similar colour. White shirts are worn with long sleeves and a white scarf is tied at the neck. A striped or red poncho is worn or folded and carried over one shoulder. On Sundays a more elaborate shirt is worn with embroidery down the front and the everyday straw hat is replaced by a broad-brimmed felt hat with a chin-strap. Boots can also be elaborate and are decorated with leather work. A buckle and strap keeps the top of the boot secure. Around the ankle the leather is pleated, a feature of Paraguayan boots, which allows extra freedom and comfort for the feet. Working boots are simple and have the minimum of decoration.

Another type of costume is based on a long-sleeved shirt worn with ankle-length trousers and boots. This is for those working on the land rather than cattle men. The shirt can be white, blue, dark blue or black, made in cotton, and can be quite plain or embroidered and decorated for special occasions. Straw hats usually accompany this costume.

PARAGUAY AND CHILE. *The woman wears a typical everyday costume of Paraguay and the man is a cowboy from Chile. The woman's skirt shows a strong Spanish background with the gathers and fullness coming from a tight-fitting basque reaching from the waist to the hips, a style similar to those worn by Spanish flamenco dancers. The skirt is made of cotton and can be patterned or plain. A very simple blouse is worn. The man, a Chilean cowboy or* huaso, *wears a costume similar in style to* horsemen in other South American countries. The huaso *wears long black gaiters or leggings. Black, brown or pin-striped trousers are tucked into the gaiters, which are worn over a black boot or shoe. Buckles fasten the gaiters at the sides and around the knees are tied bands from which hang long leather tassels. Under his square-shaped, striped poncho or* chamanto *he wears a jacket and a white shirt. Silver spurs are worn and his felt hat is kept in place with a chin-strap.*

# CHILE

THE POPULATION OF CHILE mainly consists of ethnic peoples, European immigrants and mestizo, or mixed races. The native tribes constitute a high percentage of the population, of which one of the main groups are the Araucanians.

The costume follows a similar pattern to that of other South American countries, with an adaptation of the Western style of dress. The feature of the women's costume is the wearing of a long piece of material called a *manto*, which is draped over the head, around the face, neck and shoulders in various ways. This form of head-dress can be worn over European dress or the full tribal skirts.

The Araucanians, who live in the southern provinces, weave their own material for clothing. The wool is dyed, red and dark blue being the most popular colours. The costumes have full skirts over which is worn a long-sleeved jacket or blouse. Wrapped around the shoulders and knotted in front is a shawl or blanket, or sometimes a long woollen mantle, or *ichella*.

A silver chain necklace hung with silver coins is very popular; known as a *tupu*, the shape and design is based on those worn by the Incas. Felt or straw hats are worn, but on festive days there are silver head-dresses hung with coins and tied in front with green bows.

# ARGENTINA

ARGENTINA BECAME PROSPEROUS in the nineteenth century with the development of the cattle industry. This expansion attracted Spanish and Italian immigrants, and also sheep farmers from England, Scotland and Wales.

The Argentinian women's dress is simple and is based on the pioneering style of a cotton or calico skirt and jacket. The ankle-length, full skirt had a frill at the hem and the long-sleeved jacket had a frilled basque. A large apron was worn for work and a shawl was draped around the shoulders.

The man's costume predominates and is that worn by the cowboys or gauchos who ride the vast pampas plains. The gauchos wear clothes that have evolved for horse-riding and show the ethnic love of silver and colour for decoration. Baggy cotton trousers or *bombachas* were tucked into boots or buttoned at the ankles. Around the waist was a belt called a *rastra* made of silver coins.

The jacket fastens with silver buttons and a shirt is also worn. An indispensable part of the costume is the poncho, an all-purpose garment styled like a cape or cloak. Made of sheep wool, it is dyed in various colours and used as a blanket or for protection against the weather. On special occasions an apron is worn, called a *chiripá*; this can be plain or striped and consists of a wide length of coarse woollen cloth or flannel, which is draped around the body and tucked into a belt or sash. White linen or cotton loose trousers with decorated lace hems are also worn. A black or white wide-brimmed felt hat is worn and tight-fitting riding boots, sometimes with silver spurs.

For working on the land, baggy trousers are worn with either a short boot or a type of sandal, called *ushutas*, made of rawhide or woven grass and not unlike a Spanish *alpargata* or the Italian *ciocie*.

There are many groups of indigenous people, such as the Guaranis in the north and the Pampas in the south and Patagonia. Their love of colour is shown in their woven garments and the silver earrings and brooches.

# URUGUAY

IN THE NINETEENTH CENTURY large numbers of Italians and Spaniards came to settle in Uruguay. A new culture developed and new costumes evolved, especially for the women, based on the European styles. Today folk costumes are worn only on special occasions or for folk dancing and musical presentations.

The women wear long dark, cotton skirts, gathered at the waist, under which are white petticoats. Blouses are short sleeved and cut with a boat neckline; usually of white cotton or fine linen, coloured blouses are worn on special occasions. A working costume would be in white and the only touch of colour would be a sash at the waist. The pioneering women had little time for elaborate costumes or head-dresses. The hair was plaited in two braids or made into a bun. Married women wore handkerchiefs tied under the chin. The women wore either a sandal or a lightweight shoe.

The men adapted the popular costume of the gauchos or cowboys, modelled on the style found in Argentina and other neighbouring countries. For work, loose white trousers were tucked into soft

ARGENTINA AND URUGUAY. *Both these men are cowboys; the one on the right is from Argentina and the other is a horseman from Uruguay. The Argentinian wears an everyday working costume with baggy trousers tucked into black boots and a checked shirt. He has a knotted scarf around his neck and a felt hat completes the costume. The man from Uruguay wears trousers with* *frills outside his boots and over these he wears a* chiripá, *a type of divided skirt. He has a waistcoat and a belt trimmed with coins with a white knotted scarf around his neck. Around his head he wears a protective white band, covered by a hat. He also wears soft leather boots rather than the harder high-heeled type worn by gauchos in other South American countries.*

leather boots, but for special occasions the trousers, which ended in white lace frills, were worn outside the boots. A type of red skirt called a *chiripá* was worn over these trousers and this reached from waist to calf. It was originally split up the middle, but later became much fuller, similar to a divided skirt worn over the white trousers. Red and black were mainly used with a contrasting border. With the introduction of modern saddles, the gauchos gave up wearing the *chiripá*. Still worn in some of the rural areas are the full, baggy, *bombachas* trousers in blue, black, white or grey: loose sleeveless waistcoats are also worn over white, open-necked shirts with a white or black knotted scarf round the neck. A broad leather belt trimmed with silver coins or studs, or a deep woven belt is often worn. This helps support the back during the long hours in the saddle.

The boots are of soft leather rather than the hard, high-heeled style found among the gauchos in other countries. The cattle-breeding areas are very flat, quite devoid of mountains and the gauchos need to stand in the saddle to scan the distances.

A white band used to be tied round the head over which was worn a white or black felt hat with a tall crown, but narrow brim. A chin strap keeps the hat in place. The modern gaucho no longer wears the protective white head-band but wears a wider-brimmed hat.

# INDEX

The numbers in *italics* refer to the colour illustrations. Common garments such as 'skirt', 'trousers' etc. are too numerous to list but can be seen in the illustrations.

# ACKNOWLEDGEMENTS

The author would like to thank the following who have kindly supplied material and illustrations and given up valuable time in which to discuss costumes:

Helen Wingrave, Harry Goss, Dr V. Knivett, Marjorie Barton, Doreen Bird, Roderych Lange, Betty Harvey, Joseph Hanna Khoury, Robert Ernest, Aruba Coghlan, Dale Hyde, Li Jianbo of The Embassy of the People's Republic of China, Yu Pik-yim, Lee Lee Yan, Stuart Tillotson, the *Viltis* magazine and V. Beliajus, and the Ontario *Folkdance* magazine.

Also many thanks are due to the Tourist and Information Offices of: The Netherlands, Malta, Czechoslovakia, Iran, Malaysia, Morocco, Tunisia, Iraq, Brazil, Honduras, India, Thailand, Japan and New Zealand, together with the Ceylon Tourist Board, The Tibet Society and the German Library.